Cover design by Antwan Floyd Jr.

Benjamin Thornton:

Fly Detective of Indianapolis *

By Patrick R. Pearsey

2018

"Fly Detective" was a common phrase in the 1890's to describe a detective who was sharp, in the know and not easily fooled.

Forward

Benjamin Tobias Thornton was born a slave near Winchester, Virginia in 1849. He freed himself and came to Indianapolis, Indiana where in 1876 he became one of the first African-American policemen in the city's history. He became the first and only detective of color for the Indianapolis Police Department in 1886.

While Ben Thornton is known within the Indianapolis Police Department (now known as the Indianapolis Metropolitan Police Department) for these achievements, not much more has been generally known.

In 1980 I was hired as a civilian employee by the Indianapolis Police Department (IPD). As a third generation member of it, I developed a strong interest in the department's history. In 2014 I researched the history of the African-American members of the department and found the life of Benjamin Thornton compelling. I decided to write this book the following year.

As a detective, he was recognized for his skills not only in Indianapolis but nationwide. He earned the right during his lifetime not to have "colored" printed after his name in the 19th century, apparently because it was a known fact by all and there was no need to state it after each of his exploits. Self-educated, he was described at death as the second most educated man on the department.

Patrick R. Pearsey

Note: Most of what is known of the early years of Benjamin T. Thornton, from birth to his arrival in Indiana comes from two newspaper articles, one, a detailed profile based on an interview he gave to *The Indianapolis News*, which appeared January 20, 1900. The second was his obituary which appeared June 19, 1900 in the *News*, *The Indianapolis Star* and *The Indianapolis Recorder*.

CHAPTER 1:
LIFE AS A SLAVE

Benjamin Tobias Thornton was born on December 18, 1849, within ½ mile of Winchester, Frederick County, Virginia to Tobias and Mary (Tracy) Thornton.[1] As he stated years later, "I early made the discovery that whatever advantages there might be in having been born in Virginia were heavily handicapped by my being born black and a slave."[2]

As the Civil War began in the spring of 1861, Ben found himself one of 40 or more slaves owned by a Mrs. Krebs, the daughter of a man named Gant, a large slave owner.

"Old Man Gant" as Ben referred to him in 1900, was likely Stephen J. Gant, born about 1807, who married in 1828, Frederick County, Virginia to Elizabeth Kitchen. In

---

[1] Parents names come from Indianapolis, Indiana death certificate.

[2] *The Indianapolis News*, January 20, 1900, p.9 "When I was a Boy"

1860, he owned 7 slaves in Clarke County, Virginia.[3]

Also living in Clarke County Virginia in 1860 was John Holmer Crebs, born about 1824 in Virginia. He and wife Maria owned 5 slaves that year.[4] John H. Crebs moved in 1849 to Clarke County. During the Civil War, John H. Crebs was a Sergeant in the 23rd Virginia Cavalry. In 1877 he sold his Clarke County property and returned to Winchester, Virginia, where he served as a Police Sergeant and then a Justice of the Peace, who was known to hand out punishment such as being lashed at the stake. He died July 3, 1898 in Winchester,

---

[3] 1860 Slave Schedule, Clarke Co. VA., Ancestry.com

[4] Ditto

Virginia.[5]

Tombstone of John H. Crebs – Mount Hebron Cemetery, Winchester, VA. – Findagrave.com

At the age of 12, he was hired out to work for "James Singhorse".[6] Ben recalled in 1900 that Singhorse worked three slaves, a man, a woman and Ben. The 1860 slave schedule of Frederick County, Virginia shows James A. Singhaas owning a 12 year old

---

[5] Findagrave.com

[6] James A. Singhaas, 28, listed in 1860 Frederick Co. Va. Census.

He served in the 122nd Regiment of VA. Militia.

"mulatto" female and an 8 year old "black" male.[7]

James Andrew Singhaas was born about 1832 to Christian Singhaas in Frederick County, Virginia. He married in 1851 to Mary L. Eddy and had two children, Christian W. and Annie C. Singhaas. James A. Singhaas enlisted June 18, 1861 at Berryville, Virginia in Company A of the 122nd Virginia Militia Regiment. Singhaas died July 7, 1861 according to a family record but the year seems inaccurate. He probably died in 1862-63.

Ben was ordered to plow by Singhaas. He weighed about 84 pounds and could barely swing the plow around when he came to the end of a furrow.

Singhaas had a place six miles from the town of Winchester, on the Berryville Pike. On a Saturday night in the latter part of January 1862, he said to Ben: "Tobe" (his middle name was Tobias), "If anyone in soldier clothes comes around tonight and wants to know who lives here, if he is in blue, say it's a good Union man and if in gray, say

[7] 1860 Slave Schedule, Frederick Co. VA.

Confederate. Singhaas was a man of limited loyalties but a strong desire to survive. He had been forced to join the Confederate militia as an emergency man.

The following morning, the male slave who had been working for Singhaas was missing. He had run away and left the stock unfed. Singhaas was in a bad mood and started knocking Ben about, kicking him under the chin. Around noon that day, some advance scouts of the Union army, 10 to 15 soldiers, rode up the Berryville Pike and turned into the Singhaas' lane. Singhaas greeted them very friendly. His wife and the female slave prepared dinner for the soldiers.

While the soldiers were eating, Ben began thinking about running away himself. He went into the barn and found some eggs, which he placed in his "linsey-woolsey" jacket, the first coat he'd ever had with pockets. Ben then went to the kitchen and stole some biscuits out of the oven. As he left the kitchen, Singhaas, pointing to a wheat field, said, "Tobe, go drive that cow out of the wheat."

Ben cut across the field and into the lane, running hard, not thinking about where he was going, only that he was going to get away. He ran right into a white man. "You little nigger", said the man, "I believe you are running away." Ben replied "No I isn't, I'm going on an errand for my mistress." The white man let Ben go and he came upon a "straggler", a soldier named Wells of the 16th Indiana Infantry Regiment.

Ben gave him some of his raw eggs and biscuits, which he ate readily. He repaid Ben's kindness by ordering Ben to take him to a nearby house, which unfortunately was the home of Old Man Gant, father of Ben's owner. After some questioning, Gant was satisfied that Ben belonged to his daughter and told him to go into the next room.

After several hours, Ben was let out to get something to eat. He ran through the kitchen and into some fields. According to Indianapolis Police Department historian Officer Wayne Sharp, Ben ran through the moonlight, emerging from the woods and tripped over a corpse.

He had stumbled onto a recent battlefield. Thornton swore on the spot that "he would serve his country and, therefore, honor the men who died for his freedom."[8] Ben ran through lanes and through a stream until he saw lights at the end of a road. He ran right into a line of pickets into the 14th Massachusetts, where he fell exhausted and unconscious.

Ben was taken care of by the soldiers, particularly a drummer boy about 13 years of age who was very sympathetic. They fed him and took him to their brigade commander, Colonel Pleasant A. Hackleman, of the 16th Indiana Regiment.

---

[8] Wayne Sharp, from an undated issue of the Indianapolis Journal.

[9]

General Pleasant A. Hackleman

The 16th Indiana Volunteer Infantry Regiment moved to Frederick City, Virginia on December 2, 1861. It then moved to Harper's Ferry, and later to Winchester. This is probably when runaway slave Benjamin “Tobe” was brought to them. The 16th built a bridge across the Shenandoah at Snicker's ferry, and was in various movements until Warrenton was reached in April, 1862.

Ben was relieved to see how Colonel Hackleman, who was a native of Rushville, Indiana, reacted to hearing his story of his treatment and escape. Hackleman cursed

---

[9] The Stiles E. Forsha Collection

and ordered Soldier Wells, who had returned Ben to servitude, to be taken to the guard house. Ben didn't know his name but picked him out for the Colonel out of a thousand men.

Ben became friends with Sgt. Major Oran Perry of the 16th Infantry, who had dinner with Colonel Pleasant A. Hackleman. Perry took a liking to Ben, who had waited on their table during this time.

ORAN PERRY

Vice-President "Big Five" Mining Co., Denver, Col.

Col. Oran D. Perry (1838-1929)[10]

One day, "old man Gant" came to the army camp looking for his "daughter's little nigger." Ben saw him and ran under an army tent to hide.

Gant said "We have always been Union people sah, and you have a niggah, sah, in this camp that belongs to my daughter, sah."

Colonel Hackleman replied, "I don't know a thing about you, but about all the Union people I have seen around here are the

[10] W.H. Bass Photo Company Collection, Indiana Historical Society.

soldiers and if we have got one of your niggers you will have to see the General about it."[11]

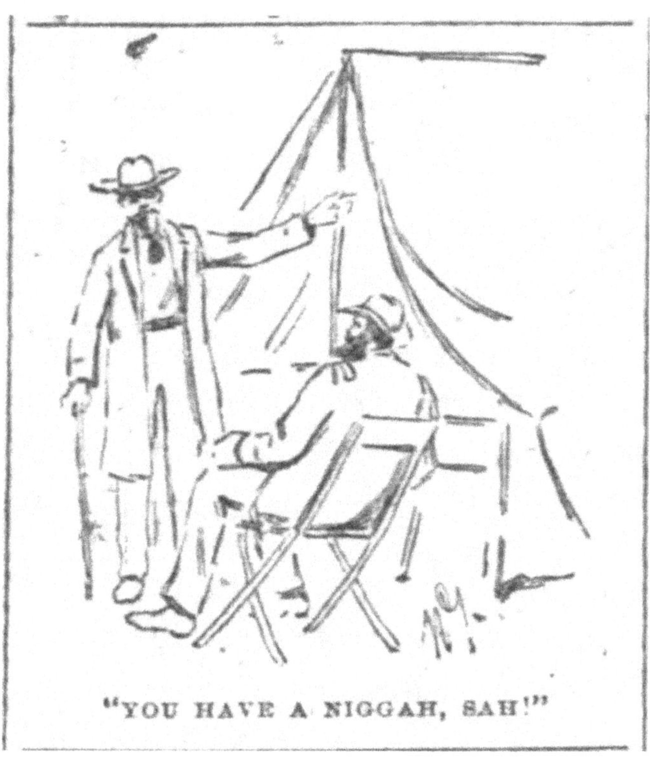

"YOU HAVE A NIGGAH, SAH!"

12

That was the last time Ben saw Mr. Gant. Col. Hackleman was commissioned a brigadier-general on April 30. The regiment was mustered out at Washington May 14, 1862, Benjamin accompanying them there, taking care of the horses.

---

[11] *The Indianapolis News* – June 19, 1894, p.2
[12] *The Indianapolis News* – June 19, 1894, p.2

Someone got Ben a job as an errand boy for the janitor at the U.S. Patent office, but he didn't take it. Ben had heard much about Richmond, Indiana. He had made several friends in the regiment who called Richmond home and was determined to stick with them.

He hopped a freight train and finally got to Richmond. Author's note: Richmond, Indiana and environs was home to many members of the Society of Friends and was friendly toward African-Americans. There were also free persons of color residing there.

His first three nights in Richmond, Ben slept in railroad cars. He had a little money that he had made in Washington, holding horses, etc. Ben purchased food each day at the restaurant at the Depot, ran by a Mr. Jewell. Mr. Jewell took notice of Ben and gave him a job. Ben worked there for two years at $25 per year.

While working at Mr. Jewell's restaurant, Ben met Jason S. Carey (1828-1884) of Indianapolis. Carey liked Ben and told him that if he was ever in need of a job, to look him up in Indianapolis, where he was going into the stove business. This meeting took place in 1864.

While in Richmond, Benjamin Thornton lived in a part of town where there were no African-Americans at that time and some white boys had it in for him. Ben was under the protection of the Starr boys and the Garr boys, who were from fine families of Richmond, but when they weren't close by, Ben had to take a chance of getting beat up. He could handle them one on one but when they ganged up on him, he'd get the worst of it.

One day, the gang chased Ben home. He jumped the fence and while protected by it, Ben threw stones at his pursuers. One of them hit a boy named Henniker in the eye. Word got back to his father that the "little nigger" had put his son's eye out and Mr. Henniker[13] came running with a revolver in hand, to kill Ben. While Henniker tumbled over the fence, Ben crawled under the house, hiding in the cellar for the next 24 hours.

---

[13] A Mr. Ananias T. Hinecker (1822-1866) lived in Wayne Co. IN.

When he emerged, a woman who lived in the house told him to stay hidden, as Henniker was still searching for him. For the next 12 hours, the woman took care of Ben, feeding him. At night he walked to Centerville, where he caught a freight train. The conductor, who had been told who Ben was, allowed him to ride to Indianapolis.

Upon arrival in Indianapolis, Indiana, Benjamin T. Thornton had $8 in his pocket, his savings for the past two years. After arriving, he met a man who listened to his story while they sat. After the man left, Ben found he had no money. This was a lesson learned. He would never let that happen to him again.

Ben stayed in Indianapolis until he was 16 years of age (1866). He worked in a cooper (carpenter) shop owned by Jason S. Carey. Carey, born in Shelby County, Ohio, November 28, 1828, came to Indianapolis from Dayton, Ohio in 1863. He was an early operator of a cooper shop in Indianapolis. He became a very successful businessman, selling stoves. He died March 28, 1894 in Indianapolis of a stroke.[14]

[15] **Jason S. Carey**

Ben then moved to Kansas City, Missouri at some time, apparently after the Civil War ended. He took a job in a cooper shop. While there, he met a young woman

[14] The Indianapolis News – March 29, 1884, p.3

[15] From "History of Indianapolis and Marion County", 1884.

named Essie M. Moore. She would become the love of Ben's life. Essie was born in Missouri in December of 1851 or 1853 to parents also born in Missouri. In 1870, Essie was employed as a domestic servant for John E. Rhodes (1831-1885), living in Cedar Falls, Black Hawk County, Iowa. He was a general agent for the McCormick Reaper Company.[16] Between 1870 and 1880, John E. Rhodes took his family to Kansas City, Jackson County, Missouri and Essie evidently came back with him.

While working at his trade as a cooper, in Kansas City, which was to make barrels, through his own efforts he obtained a fair education. Throughout his adult life, Ben Thornton was known to have excellent diction and command of the English language.

---

16 The 1870 Census of Cedar Falls Ward, Black Hawk Co. IA.

CHAPTER 2: "NO YOU WON'T KICK ME. I'M A MAN"

Ben returned to Indianapolis. On February 2, 1870, he was counted by the census taker as being 21 years of age and working as a domestic in the home of George E. Geisendorff, age 26, a salesman for a woolen factory. Geisendorff lived at 60 West Market Street, downtown Indianapolis, 1870-71.[17] Ben could read and write at that time. He later obtained a job as a bookkeeper.

On March 30, 1872, there was a large celebration of the ratification of the 15th Amendment to the Constitution on March 30, 1870.[18] This gave African-American men the right to vote. Part of the planned events was Benjamin T. Thornton reading the actual amendment at Masonic Hall. Benjamin, who only 8 years earlier was a slave with no rights, proudly read the document.

On August 2, 1872, a mass meeting of African-American citizens of Indianapolis

---

[17] 1871 Bailey's Indianapolis City Directory, p.197

[18] *The Indianapolis Journal* – March 29, 1872.

was held at the Second Baptist Church (Colored) to address a recent letter written by Senator Charles Sumner who had recently joined the Liberal Republican Party. Over 1,000 people signed a notice about the meeting including Ben Thornton.[19]

Ben Thornton found himself in an unpleasant encounter with some members of the Indianapolis police force.

On the night of Friday, July 18, 1873, Ben was walking across the "Yellow Bridge", which crossed the water canal along Indiana Avenue in company with several other men, white and black. They came upon two police officers named Taylor and Daniel Kiley cuffing and kicking a boy named Bill Turner. The officers had been sent to that location to investigate a report of a boy playing "peeping tom" at a residence at the corner of Michigan and Columbia streets.

While Ben sat on a stone, Turner walked by, crying and sniffling. Ben said to him that he should file a complaint against Patrolman Taylor, for Ben had saw the kicks administered and saw no reason for them. It

---

[19] *The Indianapolis Journal* – August 2, 1872.

turned out the officers were within hearing distance.

Taylor told Thornton to shut up and move off or he would be kicked too. Ben replied, "No you won't kick me; I'm a man" and refused to move. He was cuffed by Taylor and dragged down the street to the station house, about 5 blocks distant. Ben posted bail.

On Wednesday, July 23, 1873, the trial of Benjamin Thornton before the Mayor was held and at length he was acquitted of disturbing the peace but was fined for resisting an officer.[20]

During the trial of Officer Kiley on July 24th, evidence was presented by African-American minister the Rev. John H. Clay. He testified that he approached Officer Kiley while he was dragging Benjamin Thornton through the streets and requested the officers not to strike the prisoners. For this he was called a "God damned black son of a bitch" by Kiley.

Both Officers Kiley and Taylor were fined after pleading guilty to a charge of un-

[20] *The Indianapolis News* – July 24, 1873

officer like conduct that night. Kiley was also fined for profanity and Taylor for assault and battery on Thornton. Ben Thornton for his part was planning a damage suit for $5,000.[21]

When the Board of Police heard this case against the officers on August 3rd, it found that the officers did nothing more than the duty of their office required.[22]

When the City Council requested bids for street sprinkling, to wet down the streets, Ben submitted a bid on September 4, 1873 and got a job driving a sprinkling cart.

Ben and a few other African-American men organized a literary society in March of 1874. He was president of it.[23] In addition to becoming involved in a literary society, Ben Thornton determined to become involved in Republican politics. He attended the Center Township Republican Convention on Saturday, May 16, 1874.

The men of the township nominated the following individuals for Constable: John L.

---

[21] The Indianapolis News – July 26, 1873

[22] The Indianapolis News – August 4, 1873

[23] *The Indianapolis News* – March 28, 1874, p.3

Brown, H.B. Stewart, Jacob Biddinger, Benjamin Thornton, Frank Morris, Omer Boardman and J.S. Laney. Ben was elected by acclamation and four others were on the first ballot. Ben was listed in local newspaper ads as a candidate for Constable in August of 1874.

In an 11-man race for Constable, Ben received 8,004 votes to 8,626 for Thomas Logan. He would remain involved in local political affairs.

The Indiana Supreme Court passed down a decision on what was known as the Corey-Carter case, which upheld the principal of "separate but equal", allowing racial segregation in Indianapolis schools. Accordingly, a mass meeting was held at the Second Baptist Church on December 8, 1874 and some resolutions were drawn up.

Ben Thornton was appointed to a Finance Committee, which was directed to raise sufficient funds to defray the expenses of an appeal to the Supreme Court of the United States. Their efforts would not be successful and it would not over-turned until 1954 with Brown v. Board of Education.

Ben Thornton joined the Odd Fellows organization and on January 4, 1876, was elected one of the seven trustees of the Lincoln Union Lodge, G.U.O.F. (a Masonic Lodge).[24]

The Center Township convention was held on March 11, 1876 and again, Benjamin Thornton was nominated for township Constable, along with four other Republicans.[25] He was the only Black man on the ballot.

While waiting to see how the 1876 fall election came out, Ben Thornton knew he needed a job and he saw his opportunity with the local police department. On May 13, 1876, the city of Indianapolis hired five African-Americans as police officers, the first time they had ever done so. Two African-Americans had been hired to be turnkeys in 1873 and 1874, which meant they worked in the jail, watching over prisoners. They never patrolled the streets of Indianapolis however.

Ben Thornton submitted his application and on May 23, 1876, he was appointed

---

[24] *The Indianapolis News* – January 4, 1876, p.4

[25] *The Indianapolis News* – March 13, 1876, p.2

turnkey during the night shift for the Indianapolis Police.[26] A Democrat who held the turnkey job was forced out to make way for him and there was some grumbling about that. The Indianapolis Police force was extremely politically driven in 1876 and would be until the 1970's. You had to support the right political party to be appointed to it and hope that they stayed in power in order to avoid being replaced every year.

On May 31, 1876, Ben was appointed a Notary Public, said to be the first of his race to hold this post.[27] *The Indianapolis News* stated on June 25, 1889 that Benjamin Thornton was the first African-American man in the state of Indiana to become a Notary Public.[28]

---

[26] *The Indianapolis News* – May 24, 1876, p.4.

[27] *The Indianapolis News* – June 1, 1876, p.4

[28] *The Indianapolis News* – June 25, 1889, p.1

Headquarters of the Indianapolis Metropolitan Force, 1870-1898. It was located at the southeast corner of Alabama and Pearl Streets.

Despite being a turnkey, Ben Thornton made his first arrest in October of 1876. On September 16, 1876, a burglary[29] was committed from the firm of Maurice & Spohr shoes, 64 North Pennsylvania Street and some boots were stolen. These boots were traced to Edward Jones and Berry Robinson and they were placed under arrest by Patrolman Forbes and Benjamin Thornton.[30] Ben appeared in court November 29, 1876 as

---

[29] The Indianapolis News – September 16, 1876, p.1

[30] *The Indianapolis News* – October 30, 1876, p.4

a witness for the state in this case. The defense asserted that Ben had "bull dozed" a female witness for the defense into testifying.[31] They threatened contempt citation against Ben but as it turned out, a man named John Thornton, a local watchman, was the one who talked to the witness, not Ben Thornton.[32]

The Maurice & Spohr case was significant in that it showed the innate talent Benjamin Thornton had for police work and in particular, detective work. It would be a number of years before he could put his talents to full use however.

---

[31] *The Indianapolis News* – November 29, 1876, p.4
[32] *The Indianapolis News* – December 1, 1876, p.1

The Indiana National Bank Robbery

Interior of the Indiana National Bank at 11 E. Washington Street.[33]

On March 21, 1877, a daring bank robbery occurred at noon at the Indiana National bank, northeast corner of Meridian and Washington Streets.[34] A man carried a box into the bank, sat it down carefully, then jumped on it and used it to climb over the teller cage. He then grabbed $25,000 and was out the door in a flash. He got away.

---

[33] Indiana Historical Society: A History of the Indiana National Bank: Pioneers in Banking by Linda Weintraut and Jane R. Nolan

[34] *The Indianapolis News* – March 21, 1877, p.4

A few minutes later, two men were observed running in different directions, apparently to take attention away from the robbery suspect. They were Charles Sanford, alias Cincinnati Charley and Mike Welsh. Ben Thornton apprehended one of them and Patrolman Bisbing the other.

Both men had criminal pasts. They were convicted of having a hand in the robbery. On April 25, 1877, the ringleader of this bank robbery gang was apprehended in Norwalk, Ohio.[35] He was Harry Floyd, alias Harry Southgate. He was arraigned for this robbery May 28, 1877.[36]

Ben put in a claim for $1,000[37] of the reward the bank offered but a year later it was determined that since he was a police officer he was not eligible. To the day of his death, his part in apprehending the criminals responsible for this bank robbery was remembered as one of his highest achievements as a police officer.

Working as a turnkey required some personal risk and Ben found that out in July

---

35 *The Indianapolis News* – April 28, 1877, p.1

36 *The Indianapolis News* – May 28, 1877, p.4

37 The Indianapolis News – May 8, 1878

1877. Hattie Davis swore out a warrant on July 23, 1877 against Ben for assault and battery. She said that he gave her a black eye because she called him a "nigger". Ben countered that it was because she bit a chunk out of his anatomy and dug furrows into his face with her fingernails and he had to hit her in self-defense.[38]

Later that year in November, a prostitute named Susan Galor piled her clothes up next to the cell door and set fire to them. Ben managed to get the fire out with considerable effort.

Ben made another arrest on August 23, 1877 – this time it was Oliver Rudolph, 15 years old, suspected of burglarizing the Aughenbaugh Drug Store a few days earlier.[39]

On the evening of October 10, 1877, Benjamin Thornton and Essie Moore were wed in the Bethel A.M.E. Church of Indianapolis. The "*News*" described it as

---

[38] *The Indianapolis News* – July 23, 1877, p.4

[39] *The Indianapolis News* – August 24, 1877, p.4

being "*decidedly toney*" - meaning classy, fashionable.[40]

In early December of 1877, Ben Thornton had occasion to "threaten to chastise" Councilman Reed. This matter was brought to the attention of the Police Board to look into the turnkey's conduct on December 4th. They met on the evening of Saturday, December 8th to examine Ben Thornton on charges preferred by Mr. E.B. Reed of "un-officer like conduct and profanity." Reed also charged that Thornton had shaken his fist under Reed's nose during an encounter on Indiana Avenue and threatened him with personal chastisement "under certain contingencies."

On December 17th, the City Council met and its investigating committee reported that Turnkey Benjamin Thornton had been censured and that he had apologized to Councilman Reed and there was no further action required.

On the evening of December 24, 1877, the brutal murder of Mrs. Ida Kersey,

---

[40] *The Indianapolis News* – August 10, 1877, p.3 and August 11, 1877, p.3

occurred. The suspect was William Greenley, African-American, who had been courting her. He shot her in the street with a revolver. He was arrested two hours later. Placed in the Police jail, Ben Thornton was the turnkey on duty that night.[41]

Just after midnight, Christmas Day, 1877, a mob of people, African-Americans, approached the door to his office, which opened into an alley north of the building. The leader of the mob knocked on the door. Ben managed to recover his composure before he opened the door. He had his other hand on his mace (billy club). The leader of the mob asked if Greenley was at the station house. "He is", replied Ben. "What do you want with him?"

"We want to hang him for the murder of Ida Kersey", the leader replied, trying to force his way past Ben. Without saying a word, Ben knocked him down with his mace. Two other men who were moving toward the door, also went down under Ben's mace.

The remaining members of the mob, taken aback by the resistance shown, fled

---

[41] The Cincinnati Enquirer, December 25, 1877, p.1

down the alley. The lynch mob was masked but Ben recognized a couple of their voices.[42]

On December 26, 1877, it was announced that Ben Thornton was being moved from his position as night turnkey in the station house to walking a beat with Carter Temple Jr.[43] This would have been considered a demotion and it was probably due to his encounter with Councilman Reed. Or, perhaps they saw in Ben something more than a jailer by the way he handled the lynch mob the day before.

[42] *The Indianapolis Journal* – May 24, 1896

[43] The Indianapolis News – December 26, 1877

Carter Temple Jr., about 1890 [44]

The Indianapolis Police Department paired Patrolman Benjamin Thornton with Carter Temple Jr., who was the first African-American officer hired to walk a beat, May 13, 1874 (11 days before Ben was appointed). They started walking the 4th District

[44] Photograph property of Reginald Temple, great-grandson.

together which was along Indiana Avenue, the heart of the African-American community.

Patrolman Carter Temple Jr.

Born: November 1843 Logan County, Kentucky
Died: February 13, 1929 Indianapolis, Indiana
Date appointed to IPD: May 13, 1876
Date of Separation/Retirement: 1900
May 13, 1876: Along with four others hired this day, the first African-American police officer with the Indianapolis Police Department.

December 16, 1876: Carter Temple Jr. shot and wounded a fleeing felon named Crum Brown on Lafayette Road.
December 11, 1877: Arrested Edward Harvey, who had just shot his wife Nan three times, wounding her.
June 1, 1881: Assigned to Fourth District, along with Benjamin Thornton.
June 20, 1882: Appointed as "muscle for control of prisoners" and assigned to patrol wagon duty.

Temple was born a slave. He escaped from his master and joined the Union Army. He tried his hand at "acting" but after one performance in a minstrel show, decided to join the Indianapolis Police Department. He had already seen some action on the job.

On December 16, 1876, while tracking a man who escaped from the Marion County Jail named Crum Brown, he found him and when Brown ran, shot and wounded him. Two weeks prior to being partnered with Ben Thornton, Patrolman Temple had apprehended Edward Harvey for shooting his wife three times. She survived.

The two men had more in common than being former slaves and police officers. Both were members of the International

Organization of Odd Fellows (I.O.O.F.). They became among the wealthiest men in the African-American community of Indianapolis. While the two men apparently got along well and trusted each other as policemen, they didn't appear to socialize off duty. Temple was a Republican, as was Thornton.

Captain Warren O'Haver of the police department and Ben Thornton arrested a man named John Renihan on Election Day, October 8, 1878. He had been giving whiskey away at the third ward polls.[45]

Ben found out that a man suspected in the burglary of a home on West Washington Street had returned to Indianapolis and on October 30, 1878, arrested Henry Johnson, a barber for the crime.[46]

An example of how Patrolmen Temple and Thornton worked together in those days is found on March 20, 1879. A warrant was issued for Fred White, an African-American. He was accused of assault and battery upon Jim Ingerman. The warrant was handed to

---

[45] The Indianapolis News – October 8, 1878

[46] The Indianapolis News – October 30, 1878

Officers Temple and Thornton and on the morning of March 21st, they found their man. They were very busy so they handed him the warrant and told him to appear in the Mayor's court. Fred White did do that at 10 a.m.[47]

That same morning Ben arrested Horace T. Revels on an affidavit charging him with stealing clothing belonging to his mother's servant Mattie Garrett. Ben created a controversy in the local paper when on March 25, 1879, he saw a man stealing a chicken in an alley and fired a shot at him, the ball grazing his head. The boy claimed he was playing.[48]

---

47 *The Indianapolis News* – March 21, 1879, p.4
48 *The Indianapolis News* – March 27, 1879, p.3

CHAPTER 3: "MAY THEY LIVE LONG AND PROSPER"

On July 2, 1879, Ben Thornton was performing crowd control while firemen tried to extinguish a fire on North Mississippi Street (known as Senate Avenue after 1914). While doing so a boy named Charles Daniels refused to move back.

Thornton insisted he do so and the boy plunged a penknife blade into Thornton's left temple, causing him to bleed badly. The boy was chased by another officer for a block and a half and "soundly thumped" when apprehended.[49]

Apparently Charles Daniels had a grudge against Thornton for implicating him a month earlier in the theft of a watch. The firemen arrested him, Thornton having gone away to have his injured head sewn up. Because on July 2, 1881, President James A. Garfield was shot and ultimately died, Ben always called this his "Garfield wound."

---

[49] *The Indianapolis News* – July 3, 1879, p.4

What penalty was given Charles Daniels for assaulting Thornton isn't recorded but he was sentenced to 6 months in the county jail on December 9, 1879 for stealing two pairs of shoes from Cutting's Shoe store.[50]

Ironically, another Indianapolis Police Department officer was seriously injured the morning of July 3, 1879, Patrolman David S. Richards. He was shot during a gun battle with the "Modoc" gang and received crippling injuries. Richards and Thornton would work together on several cases in years to come.

Essie Thornton gave a farewell party on August 27, 1879 for Miss Lillie Turner. The guests were entertained by lawn croquet and music, but no dancing. She and Ben Thornton were consisted excellent hosts for parties.[51]

Essie was busy selling tickets to the Bethel AME Church festival during the fall and on October 30, 1879, the congregation gave her a copy of Chambers' Encyclopedia for selling the largest number – 245.[52]

---

[50] *The Indianapolis News* – December 9, 1879, p.1
[51] The Indianapolis Leader – August 30, 1879, p.4
[52] *The Indianapolis News* – October 31, 1879, p.4

Fred White, who Thornton and Temple had served a warrant on, March 21st, tried to rob James McMinness on the Indiana Avenue Fall Creek bridge, the night of November 16, 1879. McMinness put up a fight, injuring White's arm. The next morning, Carter Temple and Ben Thornton arrested White.[53]

The Bethel AME Church was concerned with the welfare of large numbers of African-Americans migrating to Indianapolis from the south. They had a meeting November 24th which was well attended to determine how to care for these people. Ben was elected corresponding secretary and a number of speeches were made.[54]

The following article appeared on December 6, 1879 in *The Indianapolis Journal*, praising the African-American officers who were still only on their 3rd year patrolling the city streets:

"A gentleman who was a former resident of this city, but has been out West for four or five years, and has returned for a

53 *The Indianapolis News* – November 17, 1879, p.4
54 *The Indianapolis News* – November 25, 1879, p.3

visit, remarked while passing along Indiana Avenue, 'that everything was so orderly that it did not seem to be the same old thoroughfare.' He was apprised of the fact that the avenue is under the guardianship of three of the most efficient policeman in the city, viz, Thornton, Temple and (Thomas) Hart."

Ben and Essie Thornton celebrated Christmas Day, 1879 by entertaining friends. He carved the meat and the group expressed the wish, "may they live long and prosper."[55]

Burglary Case

On Sunday, January 26, 1880 at 2 a.m., Merchant policeman William Bremer was walking his beat when he noticed the lights were off in Reese's Grocery, located at the corner of Indiana Avenue and Vermont Street. He felt something wasn't right and investigated.

Looking inside he saw two burglars at work. Feeling he needed assistance, Bremer blew several short whistles. Hearing this, Patrolmen Carter Temple Jr. and Benjamin Thornton responded to the call.

---

[55] The Indianapolis Leader – December 27, 1879

The burglars fled past Patrolman Bremer, who caught one and fired at the other. Thornton, upon his arrival, chased after the fleeing suspect. He found him leaning against a fence on Ellsworth Street, shot in the arm. The suspect, identified as Harry Stevenson, a juvenile. Taken to the hospital, Stevenson died at 6 a.m. Wednesday.[56]

In June of 1880, Ben Thornton was moved to the 2rd District for his beat. Joining him was Patrolman Henry Holt, African-American, who was a new officer.[57] The department assigned Thornton to train the new man. The two officers came across two men on at 2 a.m., July 22, 1880 trying to enter the home of Charles Haines near the corner of Alabama and Morrison Streets. Thornton grabbed one of the suspects, later identified as Charles H. Davis. The other man pointed a gun at the officers and escaped.[58]

[56] *The Indianapolis News – January 30, 1880*, p.4
[57] *The Indianapolis News – June 5, 1880*, p.4
[58] *The Indianapolis News* – July 22, 1880, p.4

Thornton Writes to the Editor

Ben read an article in the Cincinnati Enquirer on August 17, 1880 which stated that “Next Friday will be Negroes’ Day at Acton.” It further said that the preacher and the choir and everything else related to the event would be done by African-Americans.

Ben proceeded to write an editorial to the Indianapolis Leader, which appeared August 21, 1880 in which he argued that African-Americans should not be restricted to specific events on certain days, that they should be free to attend events with “white folks” on any day.

He did not believe in segregation. As he closed his lengthy editorial,

"I think it is time that our people had learned to resent such insults when presented to any body, it matters not who they are or what their standing is. If you are invited to take part in anything creditable without giving you a separate day, then go and put your best foot foremost. But if they say that Friday or any other specific day is your day, then stay as far away as you possibly can.

BENJ. THORNTON.

There was a birthday party in November, 1880, held for Captain Edward Nicholson of the Indianapolis Police Department. His wife and Essie Thornton handled [59]the arrangements at his Blackford Avenue home.

---

59 The Indianapolis Leader – November 6, 1880, p.4

CAPTAIN EDWARD W. NICHOLSON.

Mrs. Thornton gave him a gift of a fine pound glass. Nicholson received a gold badge with a bar attached bearing the inscription "Captain of Police." An eagle grasping in one talon a bunch of arrows and in the other an olive-wreath, was engraved on the badge.

On December 2, 1880, Essie hosted a masquerade party at their Bright Street home. Among the guests were Mrs. Mary

Mays, who in 1918 would become Indianapolis' first policewoman.[60]

The next time there is a record of Ben Thornton's police activities came on December 11, 1880. He had been warned that George Abbott was going to break into Herron's saloon, on Indiana Avenue. Thornton and Captain Edward Nicholson were there waiting on him.[61]

There was a meeting of the Police Board on February 5, 1881. They submitted a proposition to the police department to organize a Police Aid Association. A committee to draw up a code of bylaws was created, consisting of John A. Henry, Albert Travis, Captain McGregor, John J. Twiname and Benjamin Thornton.[62]

Handling a Drunk

When they encountered a drunk on west North Street the night of February 5, 1881, Ben and Officer Richard Wells found he refused to walk. Ben gave him a dose of "soothing syrup, while Wells pulled a street

---

[60] The Indianapolis Leader – December 4, 1880, p.4
[61] The Indianapolis News – December 11, 1880
[62] The Indianapolis Leader – February 12, 1881, p.4

car over. They then took the suspect off to the police station.[63]

A surprise 10th anniversary party was given for Mr. and Mrs. Carter Temple Jr. at their home on Minerva Street, April 15, 1881. Present were Ben and Essie Thornton among many other guests. Officer Temple was left word on his beat for him to come home at a certain hour, without explanation. He was completely surprised.[64]

On June 1, 1881, the Police Board made new appointments and assignments. Benjamin Thornton was reappointed and assigned to the Fourth District as a "Night Man", working the evening hours. His partner was Carter Temple Jr.[65]

Ben Thornton was elected to fill a vacancy on the Board of Directors of the Blake Street Building Association, the week of February 18, 1882.[66] Ben purchased a property adjoining his home the following week. He was planning making

---

[63] The Indianapolis Leader – February 12, 1881, p.4
[64] The Indianapolis Leader – April 16, 1881, p.4
[65] *The Indianapolis News* – June 2, 1881, p.3
[66] The Indianapolis Leader – February 18, 1882, p.4

improvements to it. [67] By May Ben had constructed a building there was and was going to rent it out.

Ben Thornton was a man who spoke his mind and sometimes this caused conflict. On March 31, 1882, Ben accused Constable Conrad Burley of creating discord among African-American voters. Burley denied this and then appeared to want to get physical with Thornton. Friends separated the two because they knew if Burley, who used to be the police turnkey and Thornton tangled, "it would be no child's play." [68]

There was a violent assault at Charley Ables' saloon, 336 Indiana Avenue on May 22, 1882. "Kitten" Ayres and Edward Niland entered the saloon and ordered drinks. Then they began beating Mr. Ables with a billiard cue, apparently unprovoked. Thornton and Henry Holt arrested the men and charged them with assault with intent to kill.[69]

In May of 1882, Indianapolis Police Department Chief Williamson visited Chicago to view their police patrol wagon.

---

[67] The Indianapolis Leader – February 25, 1882, p.4

[68] *The Indianapolis News* – April 1, 1882, p.1

[69] The Indianapolis Leader – May 27, 1882, p.4

Upon his return, he said he was "well pleased" with their wagon.

Shortly afterward, IPD contracted carriage maker and blacksmith Charles Black (1852-1918) to build a police patrol wagon for prisoners. Since the 1850's, the department had used wheelbarrows to transport intoxicated individuals to police headquarters.

The new wagon was built at the C.H. Black Manufacturing Company, at 44 E. Maryland St. and was made without a top. The first two officers assigned to drive it were Tim Woodruff and Peter Glazier. To supply "muscle control for the prisoners," Officers William Harness and Carter Temple were assigned to the wagon which was put into use June 19, 1882.

Ben Thornton drove the wagon on day shift in place of Carter Temple, along with Edward Harris, Samuel McClure and Henry Holt, other African-American officers.

Sometime later, protests were made due to the demoralizing effect of hauling arrested men and women through the streets in plain view. The police department assigned Black the task of creating a top for the wagon.

IPD's first police wagon in 1882

During August, 1882, the wagon made 166 trips transporting prisoners. It was replaced in March 1894.

On May 1, 1891, Black drove a motorized automobile claiming, with some justification, it was the first in the United States. He continued to build patrol wagons for IPD, as late as 1899.

A Brutal Robbery

There was a serious incident on March 12, 1883 where a Mrs. Margaret Barrett, of 910 North Delaware Street, was assaulted by a man who then robbed her house. She lay on the floor, bathed in blood due to a serious facial injury.

Ben Thornton, assisted by Captain Edward Nicholson, arrested a man named David Taylor for this crime on March 14th. He was charged with assault and battery with intent to kill and grand larceny.[70] His trial was held April 13, 1883. Taylor was found guilty and he was sentenced to 10 years in prison.[71]

The Police Department Reorganizes

The Indianapolis Police force since its organization in 1854, had been an extremely political organization. The practice since the Civil War had been for the political party in power to replace everyone on the force who wasn't a member of their party (around May 31st of the year). Then, if they lost control

---

[70] *The Indianapolis News* – March 15, 1883, p.4

[71] *The Indianapolis News* – April 13, 1883, p.4

the following year, the party that took control of Indianapolis would do the same.

This system was grossly unfair and inefficient, which is the term (inefficacy) that was used to terminate the men each year whose political party was out of power. In the spring of 1883, it was decided to change to a system where each of the major political parties had an equal number of men on the force, one Captain each, an equal number of Sergeants and Patrolmen, etc. This went as far as the number of African-Americans on the force. There were only a handful in 1883 but there had to be an equal number of Democrats and Republicans among them.

As the date of reorganizing the department, April 13, 1883 came near; much speculation in the local press was made about the fate of Benjamin T. Thornton. His reputation was already well known and although it was good, he had made a lot of enemies in the African-American area along Indiana Avenue. A number of them had been placed in jail by him over the past 6 years since he began patrolling their neighborhood. As the date of reorganization came near, both

Republicans and Democrats were pressing the Police Board to reappoint him.

Benjamin Thornton was appointed on April 13, 1883 as a member of the new Indianapolis Metropolitan Force as it was known.

Thornton received praise from the court for his work in helping solve what was called the Herman Trempe case. Three pairs of shoes had been stolen from Cromaler's store. After obtaining a search warrant, Thornton found the stolen shoes in Trempe's home. Trempe, considered a local "fence", was found guilty on May 21, 1883 and sentenced to 30 days in jail and fined $200.[72]

In the middle of November of 1883, the residence of James Hughes, the sexton of Crown Hill Cemetery was robbed by a burglar. The suspect, Warren Dunn, was arrested on November 18th by Patrolman Edward Harris and Benjamin Thornton. Dunn had in his possession Hughes' watch. A search of Dunn's room found several other

[72] The Indianapolis News – May 22, 1883, p.4

watches, which were traced to other victims of theft.[73]

Patrolman Edward Harris (1850-1908)
Date appointed to IPD: May 31, 1880
Date of Separation/Retirement: August 3, 1905 (retired)
Badge No. 82.

[73] *The Indianapolis News* – November 19, 1883, p.4

Essie Builds a Catering Business

Sometime between the years 1884-1885, Essie, Ben's wife, began operating her own catering business, out of her home at 295 Bright Street. She became very successful at it, becoming known as the best cateress in Indianapolis. There is some evidence she was the first African-American caterer in the city if not the State of Indiana. She was still operating it in 1904.

Putting in Shoe Leather

Ben Thornton spent some time working on a case of a stolen harness from Charles E. Merrifield. It was sold at auction in Noblesville, Indiana. As part of his investigation, Ben traveled to Franklin, Trafalgar and other towns, finding several sets of harness.

Thornton arrested Clemens Christy, a second-hand dealer on West Washington Street for complicity in this theft as well as others, February 26, 1884.[74] Christy was

---

[74] *The Indianapolis News* – February 26, 1884, p.4

suspected to be a "fence", dealing in stolen harnesses.

Christy went to court on March 19, 1884 during his trial, 160 stolen harnesses were brought in as evidence. He was found guilty and sentenced to three years in prison. *The Indianapolis News* singled out Patrolman Thornton for bringing the guilty party to justice in this case and the recent Trempe case and said that Judge Noble "regards Thornton as a model officer."[75]

Thornton Faces Racism

That same day, Thornton arrived on the scene where an old woman named Washington was being harassed by a group of boys. After Patrolman Thornton broke this up, Jacob McClure, White, father of one of the boys, arrived and said that no "nigger" policeman should arrest his boy.

He also used other abusive language. Thornton took hold of McClure to lead him away and while they were struggling, one of the boys struck Ben on the head and scratched his face. During this altercation,

---

[75] *The Indianapolis News* – March 19, 1884, p.4

McClure was hit on the head, falling to the ground. He alleged that Ben used his mace on him and was going to file a criminal complaint in court against him.[76]

Benjamin Thornton, although a uniformed patrolman, took the initiative to dress in plain clothes while investigating a series of thefts of chickens. After several nights dressed as a civilian and armed with a shotgun, on March 31, 1884, he came across Alonzo McClure (African-American, not related to Jacob McClure above). McClure had in his possession 18 headless chickens in a sack which he admitted he had stolen from somebody near the Brightwood area. He waived preliminary examination and looked to receive two years in prison.[77]

The Glass Ceiling

The Indianapolis News reported on February 10, 1885 that "Patrolmen Thornton, Raftery, Dawson, Roney, McCain and Harry Wheatley, as well as John Lowe, want to succeed Reed as Sergeant." [78] If Benjamin Thornton had been promoted to

---

[76] *The Indianapolis News* – February 27, 1884, p.4

[77] *The Indianapolis News* – April 1, 1884, p.4

[78] *The Indianapolis News* – February 10, 1885, p.3

Sergeant it would have been a historic moment for the Metropolitan Force.

However, he was not and that rank would not be reached by an African-American until 1918 when three men, Edward Trabue, George Sneed and Joshua Spearis were promoted. Although there was little if no opportunity to move up in the Indianapolis Police force for African-Americans, the pay was equal.

In April 1885, Ben Thornton investigated the theft of a shotgun and clothing from J.H. Stucker of New Augusta. The goods were shipped to Decatur, Illinois he determined. Ben arrived in Decatur, Illinois on the night of Sunday, May 10th. Ben arrested the guilty man, a cook named Aaron Walter of Decatur. After the arrest, he was taken away by Decatur police officers. Marshal Mason of Decatur assisted Ben in recovering the stolen property.[79]

---

[79] The Decatur (Illinois) Daily Republican – May 10, 1885

Rape Case Ends in Courtroom Drama

On Saturday, October 17, 1885, Helen Huendlind, described as "an ignorant German girl" by *The Indianapolis News*, fell into the company of a man named Harrison Tasker (or Taskell), who roomed in a stable at 626 North Pennsylvania Street. She was employed as a domestic at 635 North Meridian Street.

Tasker told Miss Huendlind that he had the address of a family looking for a servant, but he had left it in his room. She came to his room that evening as prearranged and Tasker proceeded to forcibly rape the girl. Tasker threatened her into silence with a revolver.

Huendlind jumped out of his window, falling 15 feet, twisting an ankle. Patrolman Benjamin Thornton and Edward Harris arrested Tasker on Sunday morning, who claimed she was not intimidated. He was bound over for court.[80]

[80] *The Indianapolis News* – October 19, 1885, p.1

The Marion County Court House [81]

On Wednesday, October 21, 1885, the Marion County Criminal Court room was crowded. Tasker pleaded not guilty and was ordered to jail to stand trial. Just as he was starting out the door, a shot was heard and the prisoner sank half way to the floor, being held by Officer Shaughnesy, who was blinded by the smoke and flame of the fired weapon.

The gunman attempted to fire a second time, but the pistol was knocked from his hand by Bailiff Carleton, who seized him. The man kept repeating as he was held, "Don't hold me, I won't go away. It's my

[81] www.UrbanOhio.com

sister. I did right, my mother is near crazy and so is my sister. I'll stay here." The assailant was identified as Menirod Huendlind, 19, an employee of a furniture factory.

The court doors were barred and screaming women silenced. Judge Norton left the bench to assist in restoring order. Tasker was shot in the right side, where it shattered his 9th rib and then went downward. Physicians thought the wound was fatal.

Mr. Huendlind, who spoke freely said that he determined to kill Tasker on sight after visiting his sister in bed. This was the second shooting to occur in the Marion County Court House, the first occurring in 1878.[82]

Tasker recovered from his wounds and stood trial on January 26, 1886. The first witness called was Ben Thornton.[83] On February 3, 1886, he was sentenced to 21 years in prison. In 1891 he was pardoned by

---

82 The Daily Review (Decatur, IL.) – October 22, 1885, p.1

83 *The Indianapolis News* – January 26, 1886, p.1

Indiana Governor Hovey.[84] He survived to be arrested in 1913 in the confinement of a 12 year old Louisville, Kentucky girl who hadn't been seen for two weeks after she was seen with him.[85]

Patrolman Thornton made another arrest in a sex crimes case, February 8, 1886. He charged Samuel Rosenthal with having criminal relations with Juliana White, a mentally impaired 16-year old African-American girl.[86]

On the evening of August 10, 1886, Thornton and Patrolman Joshua Spearis had occasion to arrest Harry Payton and Winston Dahorney. When they went to their room on Second Street, a pair of shoes stolen from Reissner's store was found, also a chisel which matched exactly marks made on the window frame of several establishments which had been burglarized in the past 2 weeks.

---

[84] The Huntington Democrat (Huntington, IN.) – May 7, 1891, p.2

[85] The Courier-Journal (Louisville, KY.) November 30, 1913, p.20.

[86] *The Indianapolis News* – February 8, 1886, p.1

Patrolman Joshua Spearis(1858-1945)
Date appointed to IPD: April 14, 1883

The First Detectives

On the evening of August 20, 1886, Superintendent of Police Michael O'Donnell ordered Ben to come to his office after roll call. As he recalled in 1896, Ben said, "I had no idea of what was in store for me and I supposed that I was to be 'called down', for something I had done. O'Donnell was brusque in manner and always gave his commands in a short, abrupt way. I was considerably relieved when he informed me that he could use me to greater advantage in citizens' clothes, and directed me to report for duty without my uniform the next morning."

IPD official history gives the date that Benjamin Thornton became a detective as August 25, 1886.[87]

It was believed in 1896 as Ben looked back at 10 years as a detective, that this appointment was made due to his high profile arrests of major criminals while a patrolman and his ability to go beyond this role and find clues. For a Democratic head of the police department to promote a Republican officer to this important post, says a lot.

Superintendent O'Donnell left IPD within weeks of making this ground breaking move and died in 1889 at the age of 30. He was one of the youngest heads of the

---

87 *The Indianapolis Journal* – May 24, 1896

Indianapolis Police Department in its history.

This was the first time in the Indianapolis Police Department's history that an African-American had been promoted to Detective. He may also be the first in the State of Indiana's history to hold that position in law enforcement.

For the past 8 years, Ben had solved a number of important crimes. He arrested John McClure, a man who committed a series of robberies in Kokomo, Indiana and Chicago, Illinois. He also captured the suspects in the Perkins robbery on North Mississippi Street, where a large amount of jewelry, silver and cash were stolen.[88]

He also was very familiar with the criminals in Indianapolis and their activities, which greatly aided him in solving cases. *The Indianapolis News* noted on September 16th that Patrolman Martin Haley and Thornton were detailed to special work for the city at large.[89] At this time they were the only detectives with the department.

---

[88] Ibid.

[89] *The Indianapolis News* – September 16, 1886, p.4

MARTIN HALEY.

Born: 1857 Jersey City, N.J.
Died: September 18, 1921 Indianapolis, IN.
Appointed: April 14, 1883
Removed: September 18, 1921

About 1885: Appointed to new Detective Squad.
August 18, 1885: Shot in the head by John Welch, caught in the act of burglary. Despite

his wound, which caused him pain for many years, he captured his assailant.
Left IPD for unspecified number of years.
April 1, 1889: Reappointed to IPD.
December 15, 1897: Appointed to IPD as patrolman.
January 1901: Promoted to Detective Sergeant.
April 5, 1910: Promoted from plain clothes man to Detective.
May 1921: Became ill while on vacation and was unable to return to duty.

An early burglary case Detective Ben Thornton was assigned was that of Dillman's store, 172 Indiana Avenue, which was entered by burglars on October 10, 1886. They were frightened away before they packed up much merchandise. Ben arrested two men on the following afternoon, Moses Burnett and Jerry Carmichael for the burglary.[90]

Ben Thornton would do a lot of traveling throughout the United States in pursuit of criminals and in November 1886, he went to Vermillion County, Illinois in search of Sam Dorsey. Dorsey was accused of stealing Frank Solliday's horse in 1884.

---

[90] *The Indianapolis News* – October 11, 1886, p.1

Ben found him in a coal mine there and arrested him.[91] Dorsey was sentenced to two years.

Here's how another newspaper announced his arrival in their city.

"Officer Ben Thornton, of the Indianapolis metropolitan police, was in the city yesterday after a horse thief, who was located here. Thornton is a colored man, but a very "fly" cop in his line of business. He says that in the past year fifty horses have been stolen at Indian, spoils, and not one of them recovered. Sheriff Nelson records but the loss of one horse in the past year in Allen County, and gave that thief a big chase for two days." 92

On December 14, 1886, it was announced that Detective Ben Thornton had broken up a gang of teenaged thieves, who were encouraged to steal by Abraham Sagalowsky, a junk dealer at 88 West Market Street.

They broke into vacant houses and brought him lead pipe and brasses (similar to what is occurring in the present day).

---

[91] *The Indianapolis News* – November 15, 186, p.4

[92] Fort Wayne Daily Sentinel – November 11, 1886

Thornton reported that every house on New Jersey Street, from Fort Wayne Avenue to New York Street had been stripped in the same manner.[93]

Detective Martin Haley was detailed to watch the Model store, at 41-49 E. Washington Street on Saturday evening, January 15, 1887. Several thefts of clothing had occurred there. He observed a man, later identified as Harry Brown, acting suspicious, lurking around.

When Brown tried to run, Haley captured him, finding him wearing a hat identified as belonging to a John Rosenburg. Brown admitted stealing clothing from the clothing stands at the Model, selling them to Elias Openheimer, 63 Indiana Avenue at the price of $1 per coat.

Detectives Haley and Thornton took Openheimer in charge. Their suspicions led them to the residence of Isaac Borenstein, 283 South Tennessee (later renamed Capitol) Street. There the detectives found a quantity of coats hidden in a closet. These were identified as clothing Harry Brown had

---

[93] *The Indianapolis News* – December 14, 1886, p.1

stolen and pawned to Openheimer. Also at the Borenstein residence at the time were Nathan and Samuel Borenstein. When the clothing discovery was made, they slipped out, driving a buggy rapidly to Openheimer's store.

There, they were headed off by Detective Thornton, who was a fast runner. In the end, all parties were placed under arrest. Openheimer, a brother-in-law of the Borensteins, was charged with receiving stolen goods, the others for concealing the same. The Mayor of Indianapolis discharged Nathan and Samuel on January 18th.[94]

The Arrest of John Henry Underwood

The two detectives, Ben and Martin Haley, made a major arrest on January 14, 1887. Two men named Brown and Johnson had robbed a store in Lebanon, Indiana and carted the goods to Indianapolis in a two-horse wagon. They were trying to sell the goods to a fence on East Washington Street.

---

[94] *The Indianapolis News* – January 18, 1887, p.3

Due to a disagreement, the "fence" informed the police.[95]

Detectives Benjamin Thornton and Martin Haley arrived at the pawnshop, owned by a Mr. Lauterstein. They saw a tall, well- built man handling some items that appeared to be among the stolen items they were looking for. "You've got the wrong man, I guess", he told the detectives. "We'll find out about that", replied Haley. Ben was standing in the doorway at this time, not wanting anyone to get past him.

"Well, I think you have", the tall man replied. Haley saw him pull a revolver from his coat pocket. He raised his arm and pointed the weapon at Detective Haley's chest. Haley instinctively grabbed the revolver but could not push it to the side. The man pulled the trigger, but the gun didn't fire because Haley's finger was over the hammer and between it and the cartridge.

A fierce struggle for the weapon ensued, which was joined by Ben Thornton. After several minutes, it was taken away

---

[95] *The Indianapolis News* – November 18, 1897, p.2

from the suspect, who they arrested. He laughed at the detectives. When they brought him to police headquarters, they learned the man was John Henry Underwood, a notorious burglar and hotel thief. He admitted that he wanted to kill Haley.[96]

Underwood had been a fugitive from justice for many years. He was arrested in 1881 near Indianapolis with a load of stolen goods and turned over to Boone County, Indiana officials to answer a charge of murder.

Convicted and sentenced to five years, he escaped from the sheriff in-route to the penitentiary and moved west. He and his gang robbed the Pacific express near Dallas, Texas that year. He killed a Pinkerton detective in order to escape when the rest of the gang was captured. Underwood's arrest made national news.

The Pinkerton's placed a $10,000 reward on Underwood's head. In December 1885 he was accused of murdering Israel Downing of Boone County. John Henry

---

[96] *The Indianapolis News* – April 9, 1898, p.2

Underwood was formerly a member of the famed Reno Gang of southern Indiana. "Brown", his confederate, was actually named "Walk Hammond" of Osgood, Indiana, known as "The Bandit of the Wabash", described as "mean and brutal and guilty of about every crime in the calendar." He was convicted in 1869 of robbing an O.& M. express train near Seymour, Indiana.[97] Both men were sentenced to 12 years each. Hammond died in Michigan City prison.

Shooting at the Grand Hotel

The first assault case Benjamin Thornton investigated as a detective occurred February 23, 1887 at the Grand Hotel. It was located on the southwest corner of Illinois and Tennessee Streets.

Two waiters, Thomas Lewis and Thomas Graves became involved in a quarrel which started during breakfast. Graves had taken fruit to a guest and Lewis removed it to his own table. Graves removed some of it in turn and harsh words were exchanged.

---

[97] *The Indianapolis News* – January 15, 1887, p.1

They met in the kitchen, where Graves challenged Lewis to a fight.

Graves was later terminated and after getting his pay, he met Lewis and challenged him again to fight it out. Lewis refused and as he came out of the kitchen, fired a shot at Graves, striking him near the heart, a serious wound. Lewis was arrested by Thornton at his home on 1st Street. He claimed Graves, who was a powerfully built man, had a razor and he fired in self-defense.[98] The Mayor acquitted Lewis on the basis of his self-defense claim.

IPD Officers Take Down a Wanted Suspect

Word came to the Superintendent of Police in March 1887 that Jim Benning, a fugitive from justice and reputed to be a dangerous man, was hiding in Killian's saloon. He had been arrested in Indianapolis over a year before for robbing the Hendricks County home of James W. Hughes in 1884, but after being taken to Danville, Indiana, he broke jail.

[98] *The Indianapolis News* – February 23, 1887, p.1

The Officers who Accompanied Ben:

Robert Campbell **Martin Haley**

Michael Raftery **Fred Spearing**

Sent to capture him were Captain Robert Campbell, Detectives Martin Haley and Benjamin Thornton and Patrolmen Michael Raftery and Spearing. They expected a fight due to Benning's reputation. The first officer to approach him was Thornton.

Seeing an African-American man approaching him with a grin on his face, gave him no sense of alarm and he didn't have a chance to fight. The other officers rushed in to affect the capture.[99] He received 2 years after being found guilty of the 1884 burglary, on May 12, 1887.[100]

Ben Thornton had a high level of self-confidence and this was demonstrated on March 22, 1887. He walked into 84 Wall Street and saw a crowd of nine men gambling. Ben covered the entire crowd with his revolver and made it clear what would happen if anyone tried to escape. He sent one prisoner to get the patrol wagon and another for holding the horses after the

---

[99] *The Indianapolis News* – March 14, 1887, p.1, also March 16, 1887.

[100] *The Indianapolis News* – May 12, 1887, p.1

wagon arrived. The men were fined the following morning.[101]

Thornton was known as a "money maker" and remained active in business affairs. In April 1887, he sold lots 29, 30 and 31 in St. John's west addition for $2,650 to Marshall W. Taylor, the famous bicyclist.[102] He also purchased lot 33, block 2 of Wiley & Martin's southwest addition for $675 from James M. Winter that month.[103]

A Visit to Ben's Birthplace

Late in the month of May, 1887, for reasons unknown, Ben Thornton took a trip to the Shenandoah Valley of Virginia and visited the plantation where he lived as a slave. He visited the daughter of his former owner, she being only a few years older than him. She was in fairly poor circumstances.[104]

Ben Thornton stayed busy, for example during the month of September 1887, he solved a robbery and three thefts. On October 13, 1887, two men, Owen L. Griffen

[101] *The Indianapolis News* – March 23, 1887, p.1
[102] *The Indianapolis News* – April 19, 1887, p.1
[103] *The Indianapolis News* – May 2, 1887, p.1
[104] *The Indianapolis News* – June 3, 1887, p.2

and Jack Roberts came through Indianapolis after burglarizing a store in Westfield, Indiana on October 8th. They were arrested on West Washington Street by Detectives Thornton, Haley and Bruce. Stolen property was found in their possession and they were sent to Lebanon, Indiana to face charges.[105]

Benjamin Thornton Investigates a Murder

George DeBurger, who drove the McCarty street car, was assaulted by three men about 11 p.m. on Saturday, October 22, 1887. He died at 5 a.m. October 23rd. This murder investigation was assigned to the three detectives of the Indianapolis Metropolitan Force, Martin Haley, Benjamin Thornton and Emanuel Bruce.

What little was known by October 24th was that his street car was the last one on the line for the night and there were no passengers on it when it left the turn-table near Schmidt's brewery for the stable. It was believed that the murderers ran from an alley near Delaware and Merrill Streets and started throwing rocks at the victim. One of

[105] *The Indianapolis News* – October 13, 1887, p.3

them struck DeBurger and he fell across the dash-rod on the platform. The three men ran and beat DeBurger over the head with a bar of iron and threw him over the dash of the street car under the heels of the mules.

There was a witness, 12-year old Emma Martin, who was on her way to Peter Zimmer's grocery and saw the assault, which took about 2 minutes. Conveyed to his home, DeBurger managed to say the men's faces were familiar to him and one of them was a discharged driver.

The victim was 35 years of age and had a wife and four children. Although the police found and charged two suspects who were in a saloon nearby at the time of the crime, they had alibi witnesses and were released November 2, 1887. This murder unfortunately went unsolved.[106]

Ben Thornton arrested Henry Payton on November 4, 1887 on a charge of loitering. He was actually detained however as a suspect of the robbery of $350 from R.A. Harrold, October 31st. Payton, who Thornton had arrested in 1886 for another crime,

106 The Indianapolis News – October 24, 1887, p.1

denied being anywhere near the scene of the robbery.[107] Due to a lack of evidence, he was released November 8th.

Thornton Solves a Robbery

The New York Hat Store, 4 North Pennsylvania Street was robbed and on December 5, 1887 it was announced that Detective Thornton had made arrests of the guilty parties and recovered part of the loot. Those arrested were Alfred Hathaway, alias "Dink", Sam Jones, alias "Poodle" and Edward Green, alias "Knuckles."[108] Hathaway was indicted and pled guilty on December 13, 1887.

Ben Thornton was not popular with everyone in the African-American community as has been previously stated. This as stated by *The Indianapolis News* in 1888 was "owing to the vigilance with which he has hunted down colored offenders and brought them to book."

---

[107] *The Indianapolis News* – November 5, 1887, p1
[108] *The Indianapolis News* – December 5, 1887, p.1

One person who called him to task over this issue was John L. Evans, who was a personal friend of Harrison Taskell, who Ben had arrested and testified against in a rape trial which made national news. Thornton knew that Evans would like to bring him down.

Evans was a barber and they met on January 11, 1888. Evans told Thornton that he was the enemy of their race and hinted that Thornton was guilty of a worse crime than Taskell had been. Ben demanded to know what his authority was for saying this and Evans said it was Horace Heston, African-American who used to be a turnkey at the police department.

Ben insisted that Evans meet him at Heston's shop, to which Evans agreed. That evening they met on Wall Street and stopped in the barber shop to wait for Heston. Evans renewed the argument at which point it is said Ben Thornton struck him. Evans pulled a revolver and tried to shoot, but Ben pulled the weapon away from him.

Evans had a second gun however and drew it, firing one shot. The bullet went through Ben's clothing under his right arm. The men were separated by bystanders and the incident ended.[109]

The version of events relayed to the News by Evans was that Thornton came into his barber shop and was very abusive. He accused Evans of spreading a scandalous story about him and upon learning Horace Heston was the source, he wanted them to see Heston right then. Evans said he could not go then but they agreed to meet at 9 p.m. Since Thornton had threatened violence, Evans brought two guns with him and a friend, Clay Willis.

They went to Heston's saloon on Wall Street and found Thornton there, playing cards. Evans and Wills walked to a barber shop a few doors down, followed by Thornton. There, the quarrel was renewed. Evans said that Thornton said "Somebody is going to be licked for this tonight" and I said, "Well, it won't be me."

He came up to me, put his hand on my head and pushed me and then hit me in the eye with his fist, knocked me down and hit

[109] *The Indianapolis News* – January 12, 1888, p.1

me several times after I was down. Clay pulled him off, but he still kept coming at me and I drew a pistol and tried to shoot him, but the cartridge snapped.

Clay took it from me and gave it to Thornton, because he was an officer, and then Clay and I went out west to Tennessee Street and up pretty nearly to New York. Thornton followed us, and when he came near, tried to get at me again, and then I pulled the other pistol and shot."

"He (Thornton) hit me with his mace and took the gun away and said, 'I've got both your guns. Now, you take one and I'll take the other and we'll go up this alley and fight it out.' I said, 'all right' and then he said, 'No, I'll not fight you, you are drunk. Go on home' and that was all.

He didn't arrest me and he filed no charges against me this morning. I was not drunk; I had only taken one drink, but if I was, it was his business as a policeman to arrest me and not to fight me."

This is the extent of the account of this incident by *The Indianapolis News* on January 12, 1888, no one had gotten Ben

Thornton's side of the story. Although Evans vowed to file a complaint for assault, no more of this incident is found in the local papers and apparently it ended here.

Benjamin Thornton standing in front of Police headquarters.

CHAPTER 4: "WE CAN BETTER SPARE AN OFFICER THAN A JUDGE"

At 5 p.m. on Monday, January 16, 1888, a janitor named McMillen at the post office, was asked by a clerk to deliver a small package to Judge Woods, of the Federal Court, which had just arrived. McMillen carried it to the Judge's private chamber and handed it to him.

Something about this package aroused the judge's suspicions and he carried it to the Clerk's office and summoned a couple of men who were standing nearby to investigate the contents. Among these were the District Attorney and Clerk and they also felt like Judge Woods, that while the thing may be a hoax, it would be better to turn it over to the police authorities. An officer was summonsed.

Ben Thornton arrived and was given the package. One of the men present remarked, "We can better spare a policeman than a judge of the Federal Court." At that moment Ben didn't find the remark humorous. He carried the box to Superintendent of Police Al Travis, who cut into it enough to learn that it contained two cartridges. He stopped at that point.

The examination continued the morning of January 17th. The lid was removed and it was revealed to contain a box shaped like an ordinary slate pencil box. In one end two gun cartridges, filled with powder and shot – the cartridges being marked, "U.S.C. Co., Climax, 10" – were carefully secured. Each cartridge was cut to show the powder inside, apparently to insure ignition.

On and around these cartridges powder was liberally sprinkled and resting against the shorter cartridge was a piece of sand-paper. Through the lid of the box, which slid into place, three holes were bored, through which the points of three broken matches were pushed, the ends of which, as demonstrated, had been dipped in fulminating powder. Over these holes was placed a piece of writing paper on which was written "Judge W.A. Wood."

The package was determined to be made by someone with some skills and would have blinded the judge in case of an explosion. Chief Travis took the box to a chemist named Hurty, who immediately exploded it, pronouncing it coated with fulminating powder. The judge revealed that on Saturday he had received a threatening letter, warning him to let up on a case that had been in the courts recently. If he did not, "his big carcass would be found riddled with bullets in an alley some morning." [110]

Although there was still some element of a "hoax" surrounding "the infernal machine" as it would be called, a telegram was sent to the Department of Justice, which responded to spare no expense in solving this crime. The package was sent in an official envelope of the County Clerk, Mr. Sullivan, who offered a $100 reward for the arrest and conviction of the criminal involved. Superintendent Travis stated that if the Federal Government desired, he would put Detective Thornton on the case.[111]

[110] *The Indianapolis News* – January 17, 1888, p.1
[111] *The Indianapolis News* – January 18, 1888, p.3

On January 19th Superintendent Travis gave the machine to the Federal Government and Secret Service officers began their investigation. They did not find the culprit.

DETECTIVE B. T. THORNTON,
Of Indianapolis, Ind.

Engraving from Cleveland Gazette, January 28, 1888

Murder in a Saloon

An incident occurred on March 5, 1888[112] which led to the immediate death of two men, a manhunt and death threats being made to Benjamin Thornton. It started in the saloon of Joseph Suess, 40 Malott

[112] *The Indianapolis News* - March 6, 1888, p.1

Avenue. Gus Williams had been employed there for some time. He had spent time in the Central State Insane Asylum at different times.

On March 5th, Williams was playing cards with Miller Slaughter. Nearby, Hardin Venable, age 25, was playing pool. Williams lost the card game and went to the bar. As he did, Venable laughed at him for losing the game. Williams picked up a shotgun which was kept in the bar and threatened to shoot Venable, who was still laughing.

At this point Gus Williams fired at short range, the wound blowing out a large portion of Venable's brains, killing him instantly. Williams calmly returned the gun to its resting place and left the saloon. The spectators were too paralyzed with fear to interfere.

A few moments later, Patrolman Joshua Spearis, a 5-year veteran, arrived. He began a pursuit of Williams. Patrolman Spearis was soon joined by Captain Colbert and Sergeant John Lowe. Orders were issued to capture him if possible and to shoot him if he attempted to escape, due to his

dangerous nature

John Lowe **Thomas Colbert**

Joshua Spearis

It was surmised that Gus Williams had gone to his brother Benjamin Williams' home, who lived on the alley bounded by New Jersey, East North and Walnut streets. This home was surrounded, Spearis guarding the rear, while Colbert and Lowe watched the approaches.

Spearis looked through the window and he thought he recognized Gus Williams seated inside. At this moment Colbert ordered Williams to surrender and at the same time, the man Spearis was viewing through the window sprang to his feet and made a rush for the cellar-way, down which he ran. Sergeant Lowe forced open the door and gave pursuit.

The running man later claimed that as he jumped down the cellar-way, Sergeant Lowe shot at him. When he reached the bottom, he forced the window leading to the ground floor and here he was discovered by Spearis, who fired two shots. After the second shot, the man yelled out he was hurt and offered no further attempt to escape.

As Spearis approached, the injured man yelled out, “You’ve got me!” It wasn’t until a light was brought on the scene that Spearis discovered the wrong man had attempted to escape. It was Ben Williams, not the murderer Gus Williams.

Ben Williams was brought into the home where it was found that both shots had taken effect, one of them in the right shoulder, going downward. The other entered from the rear, to the left of the spine and coming out the front of his chest.

Ben Williams made a statement that evening that said he had just returned from church and was preparing for bed when he looked out the window and saw a man standing with a cocked revolver, calling him to come out. He hadn't heard of the shooting his brother had been involved in, and, fearing violence to himself, he tried to escape and was shot at by an officer coming through the front door.

Sergeant Lowe said he didn't fire any shots so this account didn't agree with the police version. Witnesses claimed there were three shots; two very close together and a later, third shot.

While Williams' injuries were determined, Captain Colbert placed Patrolman Spearis under arrest and was sent to police headquarters. Later, the superintendent removed him from duty but he was sent home pending an investigation. Although he was not found guilty of murder, Joshua Spearis was terminated from the Metropolitan Force for this incident.

He was reappointed March 19, 1894 and served until 1934, after a distinguished career which saw him promoted to the rank of Sergeant, May 1918, the first of his race to accomplish this feat with the Indianapolis Police Department.

A Dangerous Suspect on the Loose

On March 7, 1888, Gus Williams was reported to be stalking the streets of northwest Indianapolis, making threats to several people who knew him that he would not surrender until he had killed Captain Robert Campbell and Detective Thornton of the police force, against whom he had a deadly hatred.

Williams was advised by a janitor at the Court House to surrender. He replied that there would be time enough for this after he had settled Thornton and Campbell. Both of these officers had made strong efforts to catch up with him and it was reported that they were prepared to shoot on sight.[113]

[113] The Cincinnati Enquirer – March 8, 1888

Superintendent of Police Al Travis

Citizens were either too afraid of retribution to assist police or were warning Williams of their approach. At roll call on the evening of March 7th, Superintendent Travis offered a $25 reward for information on where Williams was concealed. Sergeant Dawson increased this to $50.

The News reported on March 8th that Williams had been sighted all over Indianapolis. Captain Campbell had armed himself with a repeating rifle while Ben Thornton put his trust in a double barreled shotgun. That morning, Superintendent Travis, Captain Campbell, Sergeant Wheatley and Detectives Thornton and

Haley, as well as other officers, all in plain clothes, searched the northern quarter of the city, to no avail.

Gus Williams was captured and entered a plea of not guilty on March 16th. He was found guilty on April 5th and sentenced to life in prison.[114]

A Big Jewel Heist

In April of 1888, Nellie Coup, aged about 30, found a job as a domestic for the family of John W. Murphy. He was a former police commissioner. She fled the house on Saturday afternoon, taking with her Mrs. Murphy's gold watch, diamonds and other jewelry, value placed in excess of $1,200.

She joined her confederate, named John Philip Coup, over 45 years old. Ben learned that the man and woman had left the night before, taking with them a trunk in which she placed a package which she removed from the bosom of her dress. He found that the trunk had been sent to Cincinnati.

---

[114] *The Indianapolis News* – April 5, 1888, p.1

Detective Ben Thornton left for Cincinnati on April 23rd. They had a day's head start. It was believed that the couple was professional thieves. He then followed them to Dayton and Xenia, Ohio, where he found they had doubled back to Richmond, Indiana. Instead of going to Richmond, they went to Connersville, Indiana. From there, the woman went to Washington, Indiana and later to Southport, near Indianapolis.

Ben ended up tracing them to Vincennes, Indiana. On April 29th Ben arrested Nellie Coup in Washington, Indiana. She said that if Ben wanted to see the diamonds, he would have to see her husband, who she said was in Vincennes. He left her in the Washington jail and proceeded to Vincennes.

Ben pretended to an old man who he ran into, that he wanted to join a circus. Ben found out that Coup, an old circus man, was at a hotel in Vincennes, drunk.

At the hotel, Ben found Coup sleeping in a chair, resting his head on one hand. He crept up behind him and snapped the handcuffs on before he woke up. The diamonds were recovered, Coup telling Ben where he pawned them.[115]

He recovered $3,000 in personal property.[116] A humorous story told in 1891 about this incident says that the Vincennes Police department had been carrying around a description of Mr. Coup for a week, knew him personally and when he was brought into headquarters by Benjamin Thornton, the deputy city marshal said "Why, I have a description in my pocket that fits this man!" Indeed he did.[117]

Ben returned to Indianapolis with his prisoners on April 30th. Nellie Coup said she had been married to John Philip Coup 7 years and has had to support him. Some of the goods were pawned in Connersville.[118] On May 23rd, Mr. Coup was tried and sent to prison for nine years. Nellie Coup was sent to the reformatory for five years.[119] Breaking this jewelry theft case was one of the most

---

[115] *The Indianapolis Journal* – May 24, 1896
[116] The Fort Wayne Sentinel – April 30, 1888, p.1
[117] *The Indianapolis News* - April 6, 1891, p.5
[118] The Cincinnati Enquirer – May 1, 1888, p.5
[119] *The Indianapolis News* – May 23, 1888, p.1

notable in Ben Thornton's law enforcement career.[120]

Ben started building a home at 260 Douglass Street for $1,200 on July 13, 1888.

Thornton Breaks up a Fight

On July 26, 1888, the Indianapolis African-American democrats held a convention. After a contentious meeting, Secretary Charles H. Plummer announced there was a tie 32-32 between two candidates.

Some of the delegates accused Plummer of being a liar and scoundrel. Plummer was forced into an ante-room, where Charles Oglesby attempted to shoot him. Plummer had a gun of his own which was drawn. Five or six men could not break up this fight until Ben Thornton rushed in and placed both men under arrest, confiscating their weapons.

He started to take them to the police station, and then decided to let them go. "I am a colored Republican, said he, "and if I

---

[120] *The Indianapolis Recorder* – June 23, 1900, p.1

lock them up it will be said I did it because they were colored Democrats."[121]

The eastern part of Indianapolis had been seeing a rash of chicken thefts that summer and on the morning of August 1, 1888, the thief was spotted. Sergeant Charles Dawson and Detectives Haley and Thornton were sent to get him. The thief caught sight of Dawson and took off. The chase lasted two miles and several shots were fired by the officers. One fired by Thornton it was believed, struck the suspect in the arm or side. He got away but 17 chickens were captured.[122]

Arrest of a Murder Suspect

On August 1, 1888, Burt "Oliver" White[123], leader of a gang of youths, shot & killed Willie Ellsworth at Lafayette, Indiana. White, aged 17, was a fugitive from justice. He was hiding in Indianapolis until arrested by Detective Thornton, August 25, 1888.[124]

---

121 *The Indianapolis Journal* – July 26, 1888
122 *The Indianapolis News* – August 1, 1888, p.3
123 The Indianapolis News – February 23, 1889, p.2
124 *The Indianapolis News* – August 25, 1888, p.2

Oliver White's trial began February 23, 1889 Lafayette, Indiana. The results of this trial were not found.

On the Trail of a Watch Thief

John A. Wilkins was returning home on the Massachusetts Avenue street car on the afternoon of October 11, 1888. He was jostled by a young man and discovered after getting off that his watch had been stolen. Ben Thornton was assigned to this case.

Based on the description of the suspect provided by Mr. Wilkins, Ben arrested Charles Kinney, alias David Burns, a few hours later. He denied the theft, but said he could get the watch back if allowed his freedom.

Superintendent Travis consented to the release of Kinney from the Work House for this purpose. Kinney left Indianapolis after telling Thornton to look for the watch on Saturday.[125]

[125] The Indianapolis Journal – August 9, 1893, p.8.

Five Cops vs. Hundreds of Highwaymen

On October 19, 1888, a Democratic barbecue was held in the town of Peru, in Miami County, Indiana. Five Indianapolis Police officers were requested to supply additional security and they left for Peru on August 17th. They left with the understanding that local authorities would give them adequate assistance.

Sergeant James F. Quigley, Detective Emanuel A. Bruce, Patrolman William A. Joyce, Detective Ben Thornton and Patrolman Thomas L. Stout arrived. Captain Thomas Colbert arrived October 18th to provide good order.

Thomas L. Stout James F. Quigley

Captain Colbert upon arriving saw that there were no fewer than three hundred pickpockets and thieves, who had been drawn there from all over the country. He said that it would have taken 100 officers to have controlled them successfully. Colbert took the first train home.

The five Indianapolis police officers who stayed tried to accomplish something. From their reports later, not the slightest attention was paid to the officers of the law. The pickpockets were in such numbers that they easily resisted every attempt to suppress them.

The Indianapolis officers received little support, Ben Thornton reporting that the only help given them was one Deputy Sheriff and a Deputy Marshal. Sheriff Gray himself, of Miami County was "fool drunk" according to Thornton. That made the total force of officers seven men, five from Indianapolis.

They made a few arrests but the thieves swarmed to the point where it was too dangerous to resist them. The thieves were desperate and knew they had the upper hand. Thornton was told that if he went back to the railroad station to prevent trouble that afternoon, the pickpockets would kill him.

Sergeant Quigley, while trying to arrest a thief, threw his man to the ground and at that instant was struck in the side of the neck by a sling shot, knocking him senseless. The thieves escaped. Citizens assisted Quigley to a safe place. He was disabled for the day. The thieves left the train home at Tipton and Kokomo, having secured an immense "booty".

The Mayor of Peru sent Thornton word that the thieves had notified him of their intention to kill the Indianapolis officers if they were not called off. As he went to board the train, Ben felt a hand on his shoulder. It was Charles Kinney, the man he had released to find Mr. Wilkins' watch.

Kinney whispered to him, "Get out of this. The gang is on the train and they intend killing you." Kinney walked through the train and Ben Thornton, forewarned, prepared for trouble.

"When I went back to the station," said Thornton, "I was surrounded by a crowd of thieves. I placed my back to the wall, drew my pistol, and waited for the assault. When a trained backed up I sprang onto the rear platform. A most villainous scene was being enacted there. The platform swarmed with pickpockets. They seized an old man, bent him over, and were going through him when I interfered. I feigned to be one of them at the time and succeeded in shaming them out of the robbery of this old fellow. Presently I was identified and one of the pickpockets, a fellow who I once favored in the courts of this city (Kinney) and who remembered me, told me that I would be killed and that I had better get away. I stepped inside the car, pulled my revolver and waited for the assault. This time they came. There was one big Irishman with a knife. He led a mob of fifteen or twenty. I told them that if they stepped inside the car door the first man would die. I had my pistol pointing at them and I held them at bay."

When asked if he knew the big Irishman with a knife, Ben responded, "Yes, and if I ever meet him I'll be tempted to kill him. I never saw anything like this work yesterday and last night. Men were robbed right and left, and the thieves made no effort to conceal their purpose. On the train down here some of the cars were completely in possession of the robbers. They were highwaymen, not pickpockets. I saw them stick a revolver in one man's mouth, knock out his teeth with the muzzle, and rob him with great deliberation. Two of us (Indianapolis officers) stood back to back, threatened every instant by overwhelming numbers.

On Saturday, October 21, 1888, the gold watch stolen from John A. Wilkins arrived at IPD headquarters from Philadelphia.[126]

Showdown with U.S. Marshals

On Election Day, November 6, 1888, there was trouble in the Fourth Ward. Democrats challenged the right of African-Americans to vote early in the morning. When an affidavit was filed swearing in the vote of one of them, Democratic Inspector Jacob Bumgardner refused to receive it, stating it was not in the proper form. African-American voters were indignant and

[126] The Indianapolis Journal – October 21, 1888, p.9

they determined to swear out warrants for Bumgardner's arrest and two other Democratic election officials.

In 1888, Deputy United States Marshals were not what they are today. They were largely untrained men, hired from the local population to police the polls. For this election, over 200 marshals were appointed in Indianapolis.

There were eight Deputy United States marshals around the polls here. At one point early in the day they were about to take away Joseph Delaney, African-American, for attempting to vote, when Ben Thornton asked if there was any warrant for the man. A deputy replied that there was not and that none was necessary.

Ben replied that this man could not be taken if there was no charge against him. The Deputy Marshals became very angry and drew their revolvers, pointing them at Ben Thornton and Patrolman Charles A. Hines.

Ben Thornton looked at the deputies and told them to put their revolvers in their pockets. "If you don't", he said, "There will not be a Deputy Marshal this side of Fall

Creek in a few minutes." This was not far from the truth as feeling was starting to rise and it would have only taken a word of encouragement from Thornton to the angry African-Americans to cause a riot instantly. The Deputies obeyed Thornton's advice but were allowed to take their prisoner away.

Ben Thornton assured Delaney's friends that he would accompany the Marshal taking Delaney away and pay his bond.

Afterward, the Democrats received instructions from Captain Lang to take no man into custody without making a charge against him. Inspector Bumgardner received instructions that he could not refuse to allow a challenged vote to be sworn in. [127]

Burglary Gang Rounded Up

Otto Scarce, Ted Smith and Walter Jacobs were suspected of robbing Mrs. Henry Tutewiler's home on North Tennessee Street. Scarce was the lookout. Smith was captured the night of November 25, 1888. At noon on November 26th, Scarce and Jacobs were spotted by Ben Thornton and Patrolman

---

[127] *The Indianapolis News* – November 6, 1888, p.1

William A. Joyce on Kentucky Avenue. Jacobs was easily captured but Scarce began running. Ben pursued him closely until his wind ran out. When Scarce continued running despite Ben's commands to stop, Ben fired at Scarce's calf and brought him down. It was a slight wound.[128]

On December 13th, Walter Jacobs, Otto Scarce and Ted Smith were convicted of burglary and sentenced to a $1 fine and two years in the State's prison each.[129]

Detectives Thornton and Joyce were given the task of capturing George Hacker in December of 1888. Hacker had tried to kill James Brush, a baker on Virginia Avenue. After the assault, he fled Indianapolis, sleeping in a corn field the first night and then going to Waldron, Indiana, changing his name to Theodore Fisher.

He made a mistake in writing a letter to his landlady in Indianapolis, asking that his things be sent to the address of Theodore Fisher, Waldron. Police now had a clue. Detectives Thornton and Joyce took the

---

[128] *The Indianapolis News* – November 26, 1888, p.3
[129] *The Indianapolis News* – December 13, 1888, p.1

morning train to Shelbyville and from there took a carriage to Waldron in Shelby County. They found Hacker in bed, sound asleep. They arrested him for attempt murder, December 10th.[130]

Thornton Recovers the Governor's Watch

During the campaign for election, Governor-elect Hovey was a passenger on a train in northern Indiana. He may have been a victim of the mass pickpocketing that occurred on the train out of Peru, Indiana, on October 18th. His watch and money were stolen during that ride. Detective Thornton found the Governor's watch in possession of a man in Indianapolis; it was reported on December 19, 1888. Ben thought he had information that would lead to the recovery of nearly all of the stolen property. [131]

---

[130] *The Indianapolis News* – December 10, 1888, p.1

[131] The Fort Wayne Sentinel – December 19, 1888, p.1

CHAPTER 5: "ALL THE CROOKS ARE SORE AT THORNTON"

There was an interesting exchange in court on March 29, 1889. Henry Lautterstein was expecting a short sentence but when he appeared before Judge Irvin that morning, the judge asked, "Have you got anything to say why sentence should not be passed on you."

Lautterstein stood up and said, "Judge, I go an innocent man. I know in my heart that I am innocent. I have been a citizen of this place for nineteen years and nothing has ever been against my character. That detective (Benjamin Thornton) there is to blame Judge. I am innocent."

Prosecutor Mitchell said "All the crooks are sore at Thornton", which made Lautterstein glare at him and turn to Thornton and say, "I will get even with you yet."[132]

---

[132] *The Indianapolis News* – March 29, 1889, p.1

Ben Thornton had placed an application for Post Office Inspector and had filed a number of documents in Washington and hoped he would get an appointment in 1889. [133]

Detectives Timothy Splan and Ben Thornton arrested John Gardner, 187 Douglass Street on June 3, 1889 for grand larceny. He roomed with a co-worker, James E. Eubanks and the trunks of both men were robbed recently. The detectives accused Gardner of robbing Eubank's trunk and then breaking open his own to throw off suspicion.[134]

The week of July 28, 1889, *The Indianapolis Journal* asked several Indianapolis court house officials what the leading characteristic of the American people?

They found Ben Thornton "lounging in the corridors" and when asked the question, he seemed lost in thought. He finally said "I should say the most prominent quality in the

---

[133] *The Indianapolis News* – April 20, 1889, p.1
[134] *The Indianapolis News* – June 3, 1889, p.3

make-up of the average American is to pry into other people's business. From one end of the Nation to the other. I believe, you will find the people inquisitive, even when ambition and love of glory, and all that, is lacking. Curiosity will go pretty far in a man, and the Americans are not much behind the times in exercising it." [135]

As I Walk Into the Valley of the Shadow

There had been growing trouble at the Zion Baptist Church. There were two factions in the congregation which was over the pastor, Elder Morton. One faction wanted him to be removed and the other said that he would remain in charge of the church.

On the evening of Wednesday, July 31, 1889, John Barrett was told by his wife that Elder Morton had insulted her. Mr. Barrett took a revolver, a Colt with an 8" barrel and went up to Elder Moore's house in the afternoon, swearing that he had come to "drink the Elder's blood" and swim in ruby gore. However, he didn't do anything then.

---

[135] *The Indianapolis Journal* – July 28, 1889

At 9 p.m. that same evening, while there was a gathering at Elder Moore's home, Barrett again appeared at the door, brandishing his revolver and threatening the minister's life. Barrett was pushed out of the house and the door locked. He ran around the building trying to get in a window. The ladies that were present gathered around the Elder to protect him. Enter Detective Benjamin Thornton who marched up to Barrett and confiscated his weapon. He arrested Barrett.[136]

---

[136] *The Indianapolis News*, August 1, 1889, p.3

A scene from a 20th century western movie transpired on North Street in Indianapolis, August 9, 1889. That morning, a frightened horse dragged a wagon, almost running down several children. Ben managed to climb into the wagon and turn the horse against a fence, just in time to avoid running down an old woman.[137]

Ben Thornton went to Cincinnati and arrested John Smith, alias T. Mitchell, a piano tuner on August 11th. The "well known and 'fly' colored detective" as he was called in the Cincinnati Enquirer, was assisted by their Detectives Moses and Crawford.

---

[137] *The Indianapolis News* – August 9, 1889, p.1

Smith was charged with grand larceny for swindling Dr. W.H. Watson out of a gold watch three months prior. He stole a $50 music box in Indianapolis, traded it for a watch which he pawned for $9, then came to Cincinnati. On August 12th, Smith was bound over to a grand jury.[138] [139]

In the fall of 1889, Benjamin Thornton and other leading African-Americans, including Levi Christy and Horace Heston, felt that they had been let down by President Benjamin Harrison, ignoring them in their request for political recognition in the north. They felt their brothers in the South had been left unprotected.

They threatened to stay at home on Election Day and let the Republican party go down to defeat. These 14 men had their feelings conveyed to President Harrison on October 1, 1889 by Louis T. Michener, chairman of the Indiana State Central Committee. Michener relayed these thoughts to Elijah W. Halford, the president's private secretary.[140]

---

138 *The Indianapolis News* – August 12, 1889, p.3

139 The Cincinnati Enquirer – August 12, 1889, p.8

140 "Benjamin Harrison and the Matter of Race", The Indiana

A Trip to Denver

Word arrived that Andy Reinhart, a former employee of Edward Smith of Indianapolis, was under arrest at Denver on a charge of embezzlement. Detective Thornton left the evening of October 5, 1889 with extradition papers, to bring the prisoner back to Indiana.[141]

The Danger of Dime Novels

A 16-year old boy named Fred Owens pleaded guilty before the Mayor the morning of October 23, 1889 to stealing $200 from Dr. Charles Broich. Benjamin Thornton, assigned to the case was quoted as follows: "This is another illustration of what the reading dime novels will do for a boy."

Thornton, who made the arrest, continued, "This boy took care of Dr. Broich's horse and attended school. He ate one meal at the house and was considered a thoroughly trustworthy boy. Last Sunday

---

Magazine of History – Vol. 65, Issue 3, September 69 by George Sinkler

[141] *The Indianapolis News* – October 5, 1889, p.1

evening while the family were at supper he climbed to the second story of the house by way of the grape arbor, and took the $200 from a drawer in which he knew Dr. Broich had placed it. The boy was not suspected when the money was missed, and after I had discovered that he had been getting large coins changed and had fastened the crime on him, Mrs. Broich said she would rather give $400 than have him prosecuted. The boy had been reading yellow covered novels and the infatuation for crime so overcame him that he concluded to commit the robbery."

After Owens was arrested, he confessed the crime to Thornton. He had hidden the money in the hay loft of Dr. Broich's stable, where Thornton found $182 of it.[142]

Strongest Man in Indianapolis Murdered

A man who was reputed to be the strongest in Indianapolis was shot and killed Saturday night, November 11, 1889. There was a dance that evening at the home of Pete Burt, a driver for the Indianapolis Ice

---

[142] *The Indianapolis News* – October 23, 1889, p.1

Company. It was a small two roomed building on Michigan Road, northwest of Indianapolis.

Oscar Johnson and John Lawrence, two young men who worked in the poultry house on West Maryland Street, were in attendance. They weren't invited and were both drunk. Johnson tried to start a fight with John James, loudly declaring that he was the "best man of his inches in Indianapolis."

At the time, John James was quarreling over a girl with William English. Both Johnson and Lawrence took the side of English. Pete Burt, the host, got a revolver away from Lawrence, but gave it back on a promise that he would go home.

Johnson, Lawrence and several men and women left and went up Michigan Road to a saloon, where they drank a lot of whiskey. On their way back to the dance, Johnson and Lawrence had a fight and Lawrence fired his pistol into the air twice.

Back at the house, Lawrence decided to goad Johnson into fighting, telling him to get his gun out or he would "do" him. "The

Johnson was never born who could do me", answered Lawrence. "You can't lick me and you know it."

The two men were hustled out of the front door and to the side of the house. Johnson was using loud ugly language and Pete Burt came out and told him to be quiet. Johnson struck Burt twice and knocked him against the house. He was taken into the home by several women and the door had just closed when a shot was heard outside.

Johnson was carried into the house and placed in a chair. He lived another 20 minutes. Burt left to find the nearest telephone to call for an ambulance and the police. He met Lawrence at the end of the bridge near the home. Lawrence said "Don't you do me any dirt", slapping the pocket where he kept his pistol. Johnson died at 3:25 a.m. Sunday.

Captain Robert Campbell and Detectives Timothy Splan and Ben Thornton searched all day for Lawrence but could not find him.[143]

---

[143] *The Indianapolis News* – November 11, 1889, p.1

John Lawrence, the suspect, eluded police, being reported being seen near the Washington Street bridge on November 24, 1889.[144] It was learned later that Lawrence fled the city, going to Chicago and then to New York, finding employment on a farm. He passed through Indianapolis on his way to Louisville, Kentucky in late March, 1890. Chief of Detectives Timothy Splan sent Detective Thornton after him.

Thornton found him in a saloon, quietly watching a game of craps. After apprehending Lawrence, Ben brought him to Indianapolis at 6:30 in the evening, March 31, 1890. Although indicted for murder, the coroner was leaning toward self-defense.[145]

John Lawrence was convicted and sentenced to a term in the State Prison at Michigan City, arriving there April 25, 1890. He died there, January 31, 1893.

An argument Saturday night, December 1, 1889 occurred in a saloon on South Illinois Street. Detective Thornton was passing by and ran in to quiet things

---

[144] *The Indianapolis News* – November 25, 1889, p.2

[145] *The Indianapolis News* – April 1, 1890, p.4

down. The crowd turned on him and he was forced to pull his weapons to defend himself. The men who were fighting escaped.[146]

Ben traveled to Chicago, where on January 18, 1890 he served as one of the delegates from Indianapolis to the Afro-American League convention. Founded in 1887, the NAAL (National Afro American League)-as it was called had a goal of obtaining full citizenship and equality for African-Americans. This meeting was the first on a national level for the organization.[147] This was the first Civil Rights organization formed in the United States.

---

[146] *The Indianapolis News* – December 2, 1889, p.8

[147] Benjamin R. Justesen, Broken Brotherhood: The Rise and Fall of the National Afro-American Council (Carbondale: Southern Illinois Press, 2008) – See more at: http://www.blackpast.org/aah/national-afro-american-league-1887-1893#sthash.TMmyKrHG.dpuf

In the morning of January 27, 1890, Mrs. Charles Haeberle of 196 North Mississippi Street was preparing breakfast in the kitchen when she heard a shot. Running downstairs to the saloon her husband operated, she asked the bartender who fired the shot.

Seeing no one, he ran upstairs to the parlor and found Charles Haeberle, age 32, lying on a lounge. Dr. H.A. Denson was called. An examination of the body revealed a fatal gunshot wound on the right side of the head, above the ear.

It wasn't long before Ben Thornton and Patrolmen Seth Beem and John Hostetter, along with a News reporter, reached the scene. The dying man was found lying on a sofa-lounge with a pillow under his head. Ben found the pistol between the man's body and the left side of the lounge, partially hidden by the cover. It appeared the weapon was found a foot or so from his head and after firing the shot, had dropped the weapon across his body instead of allowing it to fall to the floor. The wife stated that he suffered a great deal from an illness and was in financial trouble.[148]

Detective Force Created

On February 1, 1890, the Indianapolis Metropolitan police formed its first organized detective force. For perhaps 20 years various people had served as "detective" for the Metropolitan Force but this was a more structured unit. The first members were:

Captain Timothy Splan, Chief of Detectives
James F. Quigley
Samuel "Billy Gerber
John W. Page
Benjamin Thornton

[148] *The Indianapolis News* – January 27, 1 890, p.1

A break-in occurred at C. Kempf's store, 206 South Meridian on the morning of February 14, 1890. Ben Thornton was detailed to investigate the case and by the next day, he had arrested James Bigham and recovered 24 razors, eight of which were in Bigham's pockets.[149]

LON HENDERSON.

Lon Henderson

By February 17, 1890, Indianapolis Metropolitan police had captured 11 burglars

---

[149] *The Indianapolis News* – February 15, 1890, p.1

and a quantity of stolen goods in a 10 day stretch. On February 16th, the home of Bryon Hutchinson, 572 North Tennessee Street was burglarized and officers arrived while the crime was in progress. The home was surrounded by Detectives Thornton, Samuel Gerber and John W. Page. Detective James F. Quigley and Chief of Detectives Timothy Splan went inside. The suspect, later identified as Lon Henderson, tried to shoot Splan, but the gun was wrestled from him and saved Splan from being shot.

James F. Quigley Timothy Splan

Ben Thornton arrested a second man, Harry Heibler, for his part in the break-in of Kempf's store, recovering five of the stolen razors on his person. Heibler tried resisting arrest, but Ben showed his weapon and got him under control.[150]

Trivia: Ben Thornton was a skilled violinist but didn't play it much by 1890.[151]

On April 9, 1890, amended articles of incorporation were filed by the Illinois & Seventh Street Saving and Loan Association.

[150] *The Indianapolis News* – February 17, 1890, p.1

[151] *The Indianapolis News* – April 4, 1890, p.4

One of the directors was Benjamin F. Thornton.[152] On March 6, 1891, Ben was elected vice-president of the board to fill the unexpired term of Mr. H.C. Tuttle.[153] One of Ben Thornton's stated goals was to provide affordable housing for African-American residents of Indianapolis. He thought Building and Loan associations operated in part by African-Americans could accomplish this.

Sheriff J.E. Edwards and Detective Webster of Lebanon, Indiana were in Indianapolis April 12, 1890, looking for three men who broke jail. They were charged with assault & battery and robbery. Chief of Detectives Timothy Splan detailed Detectives Samuel Gerber and Ben Thornton to assist the Lebanon officers in their search.[154]

On May 25, 1890, the 500 members of the Odd Fellows, African-Americans, marched from their hall on East Washington Street to the laying of a corner-stone of the Grand United Order of Odd Fellows' Temple on Indiana Avenue. The ceremony was

---

[152] *The Indianapolis News* – April 9, 1890, p.2
[153] *The Indianapolis News* – March 6, 1891, p.5
[154] *The Indianapolis News* – April 12, 1890, p.8

presided over by Carter Temple, Indianapolis police officer, master of ceremonies.

Benjamin Thornton was the principal speaker for this event. He gave what was described as an interesting speech, tracing the history of the order from their origins in America.

In his closing remarks, Ben said "We all live with the same end in view, that of relieving the wants of the distressed, burying the dead and educating the orphan. Those who were once with us, those who once grasped our hands in friendly greetings, have gone to the lodges above. They have gone to join that endless chain where there will be no separation, where God shall preside and peace shall ever reign." [155]

There was a social given at 384 West North Street on June 6, 1890. It was for the benefit of the Blackford Street Church. Two men, Jerry Wilhite and John Cooper engaged in a quarrel. Wilhite shot Cooper in the arm. It was a flesh wound. Ben Thornton arrested Wilhite, who was held on $500 bond.[156]

---

155 *The Indianapolis News* – May 26, 1 890, p.2

156 *The Indianapolis News* – June 7, 1890, p.2

The Murder of Marshal Andrew Dillon

Haughville was an independent town on the west side of Indianapolis (until 1897 when it was consolidated). Their Marshal was named Andrew Dillon. There was a dance given at Weinbrecht's Hall in Haughville Saturday night, June 21, 1890 attended by a number of African-American men and women. Trouble began after some white men engaged with the African-Americans.

Night Watchman Campbell came to Moore's Hall, where another party was going on and found Marshal Andrew Dillon. He told them he thought trouble was about to start. They went to Weinbrecht's Hall. Dillon ordered the crowd, which was creating a disturbance, to be still. One of the crowd said there was no one in Haughville who could quiet them.

Dillon said if they did not keep quiet, he would arrest them and the crowd mocked him in response. Moore and Dillon ran into the crowd and things turned violent. Dillon was kicked and knocked into a muddy gutter, but he grabbed a hold of the man who seemed to be causing the most trouble.

While Moore and Dillon walked the man away, a woman struck Dillon over the eye with a club or umbrella, opening a gash. Moore released the prisoner and threw the woman back. The crowd then closed in on the officers. Razors and sling shots were brought to bear. Several white men were in the crowd and hand to hand combat started. Dillon was again beaten and kicked.

Dillon's account later from a hospital bed said that the man he had under arrest pulled a pistol and fired one shot. Dillon pulled his own pistol, fired three times and the man he had in custody again fired and struck Dillon. The bullet struck him in the back on the left side, penetrating a lung.

[157] **Andrew Dillon**

After Dillon was taken to Dr. Cain's office. Police Surgeon Hodges arrived and removed the bullet. While this was going on, Patrick Horan was also assaulted by the crowd, slashing him on the arm with a razor. A gun was found on the ground later, which belonged to a white citizen of Haughville.

---

[157] *The Indianapolis News* – June 28, 1890, p1

The riot squad was called out by IPD and about 2 a.m., Patrolmen Hostetter and Manning arrested Pete Carpenter, African-American, at his home on McCue Street. It was charged he used the razor on Horan.

At 3 a.m. Sunday morning, Sergeant John Lowe and Patrolmen Hostetter, Manning, Kellemeyer and R.B. Smith surrounded Simon Barber's boarding house on Rhode Island Street and took from his bed Allan Ross, an African-American brick maker. He was charged for shooting Dillon, which he stoutly denied. His arrest was based on the witness account of a boy in the crowd who said he saw Ross fire the shot. [158]

Ben Thornton was described as working industriously on the shooting case since the night of June 21, 1890.[159] Marshal Dillon died from the effects of his wound at 3:15 a.m., June 28, 1890. That same morning, Allan Ross was released from jail, police being satisfied that he was innocent.[160]

---

[158] *The Indianapolis News* – June 23, 1890, p.8
[159] *The Indianapolis News* – June 23, 1890, p.2
[160] *The Indianapolis News* – June 28 ,1890, p.1

After a year of investigation which resulted in the arrest and release of several suspects, Sadie French threatened to tell all she knew of the Andrew Dillon murder, after he beat her on August 15, 1891. He then brutally beat her with a baseball bat, fracturing her skull. IPD Officer James J. Brady arrested him.

Dillon's weapon was found hidden at the home of Martha Pierce, mother of Sadie, Charles French's wife. It was recovered by Officer Edward Harris. Captain Robert Campbell Identified this gun as Dillon's as he had given it to Dillon himself.

The murder trial of Charles French began October 26, 1891. He was convicted but only sentenced to three years on a manslaughter charge. When he was convicted of assault with intent to kill Sadie French, November 3, 1891, Judge Cox sentenced him to 14-years in prison. French died at Michigan City Prison, July 4, 1894. It was felt at the time that the judge was balancing out the scales of justice.

A rash of fires occurred in Indianapolis. The last was the Antioch Church. A little girl told Ben Thornton that she saw Johnny Hampton, 9, crawl from under the church a short time before it caught fire. Ben Thornton arrested him in early July.

Upon questioning the boy, he confessed to burning the Excelsior Works, Frick's livery stable, the Antioch Church and a number of sheds. His motive was "he liked to see the fire engines run." He has held for Criminal Court.[161]

[161] *The Indianapolis News* – July 3, 1890, p.1

A CLEW IN A NUMBER.

Detective Thornton, While in Chicago, Cleverly Runs Down a Man Under Indictment Here.

Detective Thornton arrived home on Saturday from Chicago with Charles Taylor, who is under indictment for robbery committed about a year ago at a house on Munson street. Among other things taken was a gold watch, of which a description and the number were furnished to the detectives some six months ago. Detective Thornton was in Chicago recently and incidentally saw a watch which had been found on a man who had been arrested for some offense committed there. He compared the number with the number of the one stolen from the house on Munson street, and found them to be identical. He was allowed to return the watch to the owner, and bided the time when the prisoner, whose name is given above, should have served his sentence in the Chicago Bridewell. Taylor was greeted with a grand jury warrant last Friday, as he was about to leave that institution, and readily submitted to come to this city. The Chicago authorities told the detective that it was not safe to attempt to escort Taylor here alone, as he is a desperate man, but the trip was accomplished without trouble. The capture is an important one and reflects much credit upon detective Thornton.

[162]

[162] The Indianapolis Journal – July 14, 1890, p.8, https://chroniclingamerica.loc.go

Here is a brief rundown of just some of the property transactions the Thornton's executed in the 1890's. Ben's wife, Essie M. Thornton took out a building permit in her own name in July 1890. She was building a cottage at 736 North West Street for $930. Ben Thornton built a store room at 730 North West Street for $1,500 in August 1890. She also built a home at 14 Brett, for $900.[163] Essie sold lot 35 in Braden & Co.'s addition for $400 to J.C. Duran. This was all during the month of July 1890.[164]

Benjamin Thornton laid out two additions for the city of Indianapolis. One was on the northwest corner of 13th & West Streets comprising 8 lots called Thornton's West Street Addition. The other was on the southeast corner of 15th Street and Mill Street and was called "Thornton's Sub." From the plat at 13th and West he made these transactions:

[163] *The Indianapolis News* – July 21, 1890, p.3
[164] *The Indianapolis News* – July 28, 1890, p.3

- June 1890: Sold lot 8 to Thomas Bowman for $1,100. (518 West 13th Street).
- November 1890: Sold lot 1 for $2,700 to Samuel F. Herron. This became 1302 North West Street which is a home in 2015. Herron had served the Indianapolis police department from 1879-1880.
- August 1892: Purchased lot 2 for $1,296 from George A. Richardson.
- November 1892: Purchased lot 6 for $1,000 from Andrew Johnson.
- ?? Sold Lot 4 for $1,500 to Seymour Miller.[165] (1310 North West Street).
- June 1894: Essie M. Thornton purchased lot 6 from Martha B. Miles for $1,000. (514 West 13th Street).
- July 1895: Sold lot 2 for $1,300 to William H. White. (1306 North West Street).

The other tract of 7 lots at 15th and Mill Streets was taken over during the construction of I-65 in the 1960's.

Essie's Family Ties

On August 22, 1890, Essie Thornton had dinner in Saint Paul, Minnesota at the

[165] *The Indianapolis News* – August 16, 1890, p.2

home of Miss Rebecca Moore. Rebecca may have been a sister or niece. Very little is known of Essie's family unfortunately.[166]

Ben Thornton was assigned to investigate a violent robbery case on October 13, 1890. At 3 a.m. that day, Robert Middleton, a Big Four Railroad operator looked up from his desk and saw a man with a handkerchief tied around his face. At that same moment the man fired a gun through the window, striking Middleton in the leg. It was a flesh wound and he fell to the ground.

The man at the window, thinking the victim dead, entered and stole a watch and money from his pockets, then left.[167] This case was never solved as far as can be determined.

Murder on Ohio Street

On August 18, 1890, a murder occurred in the saloon of Emanuel Collins, on Ohio Street, corner of Columbia alley. William J. Roberts was a young man who tended bar.

---

166 The Appeal, Saint Paul, Minnesota, August 23, 1890, p.1

167 *The Indianapolis News* – October 13, 1890, p.2

Just before 11 p.m., John Coleman, described as a desperado and who was strongly suspected of the murder in June of Marshal Andrew Dillon, came into the saloon. He was drunk and acting mean. He demanded that Roberts pay him $1.25, which he said he didn't owe him.

Some words were exchanged and Coleman drew a pistol and fired, striking Roberts in the stomach. He died on the way to the hospital from the wound. The killer fled to Lebanon, Indiana, where the Marshal tried to arrest him but he was knocked down and injured by Coleman. He was said to have boarded a freight train in Indianapolis and was in Chicago not long afterward.[168]

Coleman admitted later that he went to St. Louis, where he was working as a roustabout. The St. Louis police were tipped off to his presence by a man working for Ben Thornton, who had been assigned to the case. He was paid $50 from Thornton for this information.

When Thornton returned to Indianapolis' Union Station the afternoon of

---

[168] *The Indianapolis News* – August 18, 1890, p.4

October 17, 1890, there was a large crowd of angry people from the African-American community waiting. They had taken a strong interest in the case since the murder, as William Roberts was an inoffensive man, sick with TB.

Threats were made against Thornton's prisoner and he hustled him to the Police Station House as soon as possible.[169] On February 1, 1891, John Coleman was sentenced to life in prison for murder. He died there, August 15, 1896.

---

[169] *The Indianapolis News* – October 18, 1890, p.8

Benjamin T. Thornton in uniform, 1890

Detectives Thornton and John W. Page gave chase the evening of November 12, 1890 of a young man they suspected of stealing former Mayor Grubb's overcoat. They caught him and found in his pockets a pair of stolen gloves.

The next morning the detectives recovered items that had been stolen from various rooms around town, including the

English Hotel. While the arrested man, John Roach was in jail, a young lady called to see him, saying they were to be married the following Tuesday. Superintendent Al Travis advised her to postpone the marriage for a year or two.[170] Roach spent December 6, 1890 to November 6, 1891 in the State Prison.

The Metropolitan Club elected Benjamin T. Thornton its president on January 9, 1891.[171]

Thornton's Daughter is Kidnapped

A strange thing happened on January 18, 1891. A little girl named Ethel Mosby had been awarded to the Board of Children's Guardians by Judge Taylor. Ben and Essie Thornton had then adopted the girl who was then in the Colored Guardian's Home.

After the judge's decision, Mrs. Mattie Holly and Mrs. Ella Mosby, the mother, went to the Thornton home. While Mrs. Mosby talked with Mrs. Thornton, the Holly woman stole the child.

---

[170] *The Indianapolis News* – November 12, 1 890, p1

[171] *The Indianapolis News* – January 10, 1891, p.2

Benjamin Thornton was notified and after a search of the neighborhood, found the child hidden in the home of one of the witnesses and took her back home. Mrs. Holly could not be immediately located but a warrant was sworn out for child stealing for her.[172]

It is believed that Ethel Mosby's name was changed soon afterward to Adelaide Thornton. Adelaide, who made national news in 1894, was referred on one occasion as a foster child of Ben and Essie Thornton. If she was, "Addie" was never treated as one. She was very much loved by her new parents.

Serial Arsonist at Work

There was a rash of fires in town during the last half of August 1891, which Indianapolis police officials were satisfied were the work of an arsonist. One clue was that a man on a white horse and red wagon had been seen in the vicinity of the burned barns just before the fires.

---

[172] *The Indianapolis News* – January 19, 1891, p.1

On the evening of August 24, 1891, Detectives Thornton and John W. Page brought in the horse, wagon and driver suspected to have been seen at these fire scenes. The man gave his name as John Taylor, 66 Arizona Street. He said he was a carpenter. Some matches were found on him. He vehemently denied any role in the fires.

A man was seen also on the night of August 24th, trying to set fire to the shed at the rear of 32 School Street. He was chased but made his escape. Another instance that night was reported of a man trying to set fire to a stable at the back of 21 Fletcher Avenue. He also got away.[173]

---

[173] *The Indianapolis News* – August 25, 1891, p.5

CHAPTER 6: "I PROPOSE TO PROTECT THESE MEN IF I CAN"

The "Yellow Bridge"

One of Benjamin T. Thornton's finest moments came on October 5, 1891. A political rally for African-Americans was being held on the "Yellow Bridge" across the canal on Indiana Avenue. A platform had been erected on the bridge. Three African-American men were scheduled to speak to the crowd; James Hill, attorney; A.E. Manning, deputy county clerk and L.A. Simpson, of the Indianapolis Freeman newspaper.

Word had come out earlier in the evening by the "Bucktown Beavers" gang (made up of African-American youths),that "no Sullivan niggers could talk" and there would be trouble if they attempted to. It was alleged later that alcohol was provided to the "Bucktown Beavers" to get them liquored up and to "have fun" with the speakers.

There were about 1,000 people present, mostly African-American and a number were drunk according to *The Indianapolis News*. James Hill was the first scheduled speaker and he was greeted with howls and profanity by the crowd, who pelted him with mud. Some stones were thrown at him as well. He kept on talking. A shower of eggs came as he sat down.

The uproar from the crowd became so great that Detective Ben Thornton mounted the podium and urged the people to either be quiet or to leave. "This is a free country," he said, "and these men have a right to speak here. Give them fair play. I am as good a Republican as any man in this crowd, but I propose to protect these men if I can, and if I am compelled to do so I will take a hand myself in defense of free speech."

Ben's remarks were greeted by yelling and curses and as he climbed down, a shower of stones was hurled at him. None hit him. James Hill saw an opportunity to get away and buttoning up his coat, made his way through the crowd. He was spotted and a yell came out, "There he is now, there goes the ______." Hill, hearing this, began rushing while a mob of over 200 people howling came after him. Hill managed to escape.

Mr. A.E. Manning meanwhile had mounted the podium, trying to speak. He was hit by an over-ripe egg, then he vanished. No one saw where he went. Mr. L.A. Simpson got the worst of it.

He got more abuse from the drunken crowd than the other two. Giving up an attempt to speak, he waved his hand and started stepping down the platform. The mob threw one bunch of stones after another and made a rush for him. Razors were flashing and uniforms worn by Indianapolis police officers Martin Hyland and John Manning were "cut into ribbons." Some in the crowd were grabbing at the officers.

Detective Thornton caught one of the arms of L.A. Simpson, who was trembling with fright. Two policemen were in front of Simpson and Captain James F. Quigley followed from behind. The mob started to close in and Detective Thornton ordered them back. They shouted, "Give it to him, "kill the _____", "knock Thornton's head off" to quote a few.

Ben Thornton pulled his pistol and ordered the crowd back again and when they tried to close in on him he fired his pistol in the air. The mob fell over each other trying to get away at this point. Recovering, they again charged and once again Thornton fired into the air, stating that the next one would be into the crowd.

Captain Charles F. Dawson and a squad of police finally succeeded in forcing back the crowd and took him to the English Hotel by an around about route, to safety. Superintendent Thomas Colbert arrived to take charge and a police patrol wagon dashed into the crowd. Patrolman Adolph Asch arrested William Lewis.

Charles Dawson

_John Kaehn **_Adolph Asch**

A number of persons were struck by stones, Captain Quigley's hat was knocked off and Detective Kaehn was struck in the face. No serious injuries occurred. *The Indianapolis News* stated "Detective

Thornton's bravery was complimented on all sides" and "Detective Ben Thornton's bravery had much to do with preventing murder." [174] For his part, Thornton was busy trying to locate the ringleaders of the mob.

Jeremiah Kinney

Born: March 28, 1865 Indianapolis, IN.
Died: June 9, 1931 Indianapolis, IN.
Appointed: June 21, 1887
Separated: June 9, 1931 (His death)

April 15, 1889: Reappointed to force.
November 5, 1891: Promoted to Detective Squad.
December 15, 1899: Appointed Captain of Detectives.

---

[174] *The Indianapolis News* – October 6, 1891, p.8

As a detective, developed the art of taking mug shots and after visiting other cities to study the Bertillon system, brought it to IPD.

August 3, 1903: Chester Weekley, fraud suspect fled from police headquarters after being questioned. While running through the nearby Monon R.R. yard, Det. Jerry Kinney shot him once through the arm, which stopped his flight.

Lieutenant of Detectives during Mayor Bell administration.
October 21, 1903: Promoted to Captain of Detective Division.
January 3, 1906: Reduced from Captain of Detective Division to Detective.
February 17, 1909: Promoted to Lieutenant.
March 23, 1910: Promoted to Lieutenant of Detectives.
Inspector of Detectives during Jewett administration
August 1, 1919: Appointed Chief of Police.
August 28, 1922: Captain of Detectives.
June 9, 1931: Serving again as Chief of Police when he died.
Buried Holy Cross Cemetery.

Ben Thornton's Partners

On November 5, 1891, Patrolmen Jerry Kinney and Samuel James were promoted to the detective force. They were on a 30 day trial and if they fit in well, would be made plain clothes men permanently. Samuel James would be partners with Ben Thornton many times in 1892-1893.[175]

"Jerry" Kinney would become partners with Ben Thornton for a long time and were a team to be feared by criminals in Indianapolis. Their early association was one that as Kinney rose to the top of the department, he never forgot Ben Thornton.

It should be noted that for some time now, the Indianapolis papers had ceased referring to Benjamin Thornton as "colored" except as when it was important to the story, such as the riot on Yellow Bridge. This is extremely rare for any newspaper in the 1890's.

There had been a robbery on South Meridian Street on November 13, 1891. George Snovels robbed August Rhake in his room of a diamond solitaire and a gold watch,

---

175 *The Indianapolis News* – November 6, 1891, p.2

total value of $195. Ben Thornton was assigned to the case, which took him to Louisville, Kentucky. The watch was pawned in Louisville, where Ben caught the suspect. The diamond was recovered from an Indianapolis pawn shop.[176] George Snovels, 18, appeared in Criminal Court, January 5, 1892. He confessed to the crime and was sentenced to 90 days in the work-house and a fine of $1 and costs. It was his first offense.[177]

A nine-year old girl was molested on the night of November 27, 1891. The following morning, Patrolman Martin McGuff, who worked hard on this case, saw the suspect and chased after him. McGuff apprehended the man, Charles "the Cowboy" Bisso, a man who dressed in cowboy garb and known as a tough customer.

---

[176] *The Indianapolis Journal* – November 25, 1891

[177] *The Indianapolis News* – January 5, 1892, p.2

Martin McGuff

As word got around why police had arrested Bisso, a number of citizens arrived with the intent of lynching him. McGuff was forced to display his revolver to save the prisoner. At Michigan and Noble Streets, while waiting for the wagon, the crowd tried to get to the prisoner again. Patrolmen J. Richardson and T.J. Simpson arrived and soon were joined by Detectives Ben Thornton and Samuel James. The officers persuaded the enraged citizens to let the law handle it.

Bisso finally admitted his guilt to the detectives. He also admitted to attacking another young girl several months previous. The girl was listed in critical condition on November 28th.[178] Angry crowds were present in court November 30th as he plead guilty and who followed the suspect from the court across the street to the jail. Only the presence of Indianapolis police officers kept them back.

That night at 11 p.m., men began gathering just opposite the jail. The jail officers became apprehensive and phoned the police. By the time they arrived, the jail approaches were blocked by the mob. By midnight about 300 persons were around the jail, some on top of it.

After three calls to the sheriff to be allowed entry that went unanswered, the mob began to hammer down the door. Finally a crowbar was used and the heavy iron door fell with a crash. The turnkey was overpowered and the keys taken from him.

---

[178] *The Indianapolis News* – November 28, 1891, p.2

An announcement being made on the outside that the door was breached, 20 police officers who had been called from their beats rushed into the jail from the east entrance, which the mob had left unguarded. They went to the other side and were face to face with them.

After a moment of silence from the mob, seeing the officers, they began abusing the officers in the "vilest terms". Above this on the second floor, part of the mob was trying to open Bisson's cell door and upon learning the police were in the building, lost all their courage.

One by one they left and as the last one departed, the police blocked the door to prevent any further attempts to get at Bisson. By 3 a.m. the jail was securely guarded.[179] Bisso was sentenced to 21 years in prison on December 9th for his crime.[180] Bisso was paroled Sepember 14, 1903.

On Sunday morning, about 2 a.m., January 3, 1892, a man used a brick to break a window in the Model clothing store on

---

[179] The Daily Democrat (Huntington, IN.) – December 1, 1891, p.1

[180] The Warren (Minnesota) Sheaf – December 9, 1891, p.2

Pennsylvania Street. He crawled in and dressed himself in a brand new outfit. He left his old clothes on the floor. Inside the old coat was a letter to the suspect, Robert Wilson from his sweetheart, telling him to answer to an address on Patterson Street.

About 4 p.m. January 4th, Detectives Ben Thornton and Samuel James rushed into 186 Patterson Street and found their man. The police covered him with their revolvers and he surrendered. He admitted his guilt the following morning.[181]

Conducting Surveillance

John T. Budenz was one of the best known young men in Indianapolis. For many years he had been a trusted bookkeeper for the L.S. Ayres & Company store here. In response however to rumors that there was a shortage in the company books, the Indianapolis Police detailed Detective Thornton to covertly watch Mr. Budenz, who was staying at the Grand Hotel.

Thornton was careful that Budenz had no idea he was being watched. On January 29, 1892, Chief of Detectives Timothy Splan

---

[181] *The Indianapolis News* – January 4, 1892, p.3

and Superintendent Thomas Colbert learned that *The Indianapolis News* knew about the subject and was going to print it. Ben was instructed to let Budenz know he was under surveillance, which he did.

Ben stayed in room 53 of the Grand Hotel, keeping the room of Budenz in view. He declined to speak to the News reporter when he called on Budenz, who also refused to talk.[182] Since the superintendent called off the surveillance on January 31st, since Budenz had not attempted to leave town, this is where the matter ended.

Thornton's Thoughts on Rehabilitation

An Indianapolis News reporter spent the night at the police station house for a story. He interviewed Ben Thornton, who gave his opinion on the reformation of criminals. "A good many plays are on the stage and books are written wherein the hero is an ex-convict and will not be allowed to lead an honest life because the officers are generally watching them. A good deal of this stuff is rot", Thornton said.

---

[182] *The Indianapolis News* – January 30, 1 892, p.7

He continued, "Occasionally a man after a term in prison reforms, but eight out of ten do not. I believe always in giving a man a chance, but I always keep my eye on an ex-convict, though I never reported one of them to a man who employed him. A man may violate a law when drunk who would not do so sober. There is some chance for him – not much for the chap who steals rather than work." [183]

"Ft. Dodge" was a small, broken down frame building, located south of Second Street and west of the railroad. It was a meeting place for various men, many of whom were known chicken thieves. Inside were drums, old guns, sabers and many chicken feathers.

On February 8, 1892, Detectives Ben Thornton and Samuel James were sure that at the "garrison" at Ft. Dodge were the ones who had stolen so many chickens in Indianapolis lately. They arrested seven men.[184]

---

183 *The Indianapolis News* – January 30, 1892, p.12

184 *The Indianapolis News* – February 8, 1892, p.6

Benjamin Thornton vs. School Teachers

A meeting was held at Simpson Chapel, corner of Second and Howard Streets on February 22, 1892.[185] About 250 African-Americans met there to discuss charges made against two young women, Misses Victoria and Mary Wilson, who had recently been promoted to the rank of principal of schools No. 18 and No. 23. Both were African-American women but were light enough in complexion so they could pass for White. They had worked in the local schools for 16 years.

The women, who were present, were charged with "letting the colored school on the south side die down", with attending a white church, with not affiliating themselves with the African-American race and finally, Victoria Wilson called a student "a little nappy headed 'nigger'."

Ben Thornton's position was against the women and he charged that they attended a "pro-slavery church", meaning St. Paul's cathedral. He recommended that a committee of five be appointed to go before

---

185 *The Indianapolis News* – February 23, 1892, p.3

the School Board and demanded the removal of the ladies.

William W. Christy, who was a leading man in the community, defended the women and blamed the charges on failed seekers of the principal's office. Christy's daughter Emma, then aged 27, would become the first African-American policewoman in the state of Indiana in 1918.

His other daughter, Cora Christy, became a career teacher in Indianapolis public schools. In the end, Thornton was appointed to the committee of five. The effort to remove the women failed and in May of 1892 both were employed as principals.[186]

Shortly after the meeting, someone approached Ben Thornton and offered $50 to each of the committee members to drop the matter. He said $500 would not be enough.[187]

Detective Samuel James was the partner of Ben Thornton throughout the year of 1892. The two men were assigned to a safe breaking case on March 18, 1892. The

[186] *The Indianapolis News* – May 6, 1892, p.5
[187] *The Indianapolis News* – March 28, 1892, p.1

large safe at Francke & Schindler, hardware dealers at 35 South Meridian Street was broken into the night before. After a close examination of the safe, the detectives were confident it was the work of a professional but found no clues.[188]

Ben Thornton was a long-time supporter of the idea of Building and Loan companies in the African-American community. On March 23, 1892, the Colored Building Association, a meeting of colored business men and citizens was held at the undertaking establishment of C. M. C. Willis, on Indiana Avenue.

They organized the Fidelity Building and Loan Association, with a capital stock of $900,000. The board of directors was composed of C. A. Webb, W. W. Christy, Anderson Lewis, G. L. Jones, F. K. Allen. W. M. Lewis. Charles Rogers, C. M. C. Willis and Benjamin Thornton.[189]

The Chinese business in the Cleveland Block, of Pang Yim, selling tea and dragon

---

[188] *The Indianapolis News* – March 18, 1892, p.2

[189] *The Indianapolis News* – March 24, 1892

decorated rugs and screens was discovered burned just before 11 p.m. on March 30, 1892. The fire was suppressed by the fire department, loss at $300. Between 1 and 2 a.m. on March 31, 1892, it was once again discovered burning. This time, the fire was an apparent arson, loss of $800, store badly wrecked.[190]

Later in the day, Ben Thornton and Samuel James of the police department had arrested him for arson. They were placed on this case after the second fire at Pang Yim's place. He left the store only 17 minutes prior to the first fire. Pang Yim, who famously married American girl weeks earlier, said resentment from fellow Chinese led to the arson. [191] There is no record of this case going to court.

Ben and Essie threw a party to celebrate their daughter Adelaide "Addie" Thornton's 4th birthday, May 20, 1892. They served an elaborate luncheon and the house was decorated appropriately. Twenty-four

---

[190] The Cincinnati Enquirer – April 1, 1892, p.4

[191] *The Indianapolis News* – April 1, 1892, p.2

children attended. Among her gifts received were a tricycle and a gold ring.[192]

The home of John Browning on St. Clair Street was broken into. George Vorhees was arrested May 27, 1892 by Ben Thornton for the crime.[193]

Working for Benjamin Harrison

The Indianapolis News reported on June 7, 1892 that "Ben Thornton is at the head of a force of colored detectives employed by the Harrison managers to watch "the coons", as they are usually styled by the Republican politicians here. Thornton is a pretty good detective but he has the biggest contract on his hands that he has ever undertaken."[194]

This appointment was made was at the national Republican Convention at Minneapolis, Minnesota. Thornton attended the Convention as a delegate supporting James G. Blaine. Ben was quoted about his

---

[192] *The Indianapolis Journal* – May 22, 1892
[193] *The Indianapolis News* – May 27, 1892, p.2
[194] *The Indianapolis News* – June 7, 1892, p.1

feelings regarding the nominee, Benjamin Harrison: "I am satisfied." [195]

The Indianapolis News ran a short profile of Benjamin T. Thornton on June 11, 1892. It was part of a story on the most prosperous African-Americans in Indianapolis. In it, it described him as a detective on the police force, said to be worth nearly $10,000. Well known to the general public here and elsewhere.

He resided at 295 Bright Street and owns a number of valuable pieces of property in Indianapolis. He was instrumental in the building of the Colored Odd Fellows' Hall on Indiana Avenue. His wife has property in her own name.[196]

A dead baby was found lying next to the railroad tracks of the Cincinnati, Hamilton and Dayton Railroad, the morning of July 30, 1892. A heavy blow to the forehead was the likely cause of death according to Coroner Manker, who felt homicide was the cause of death.

---

[195] *The Indianapolis News* – June 10, 1892, p.1
[196] *The Indianapolis News* – June 11, 1892, p.12

The child was well dressed and about 3 weeks old, male and white. Detectives Ben Thornton and Samuel James were assigned to the case.[197] There is no evidence this case was solved.

On the morning of August 8, 1892, Joseph Marchman ran off with a bag of money from White Brothers' grocery on Indiana Avenue. He was captured by Ben Thornton after a "hard chase." The money was recovered.[198]

On the morning of August 13, 1892, Ben Thornton boarded a train for Cincinnati. He was going to pick up a prisoner held by police there named Jesse Linson of Indianapolis. A month earlier, Linson had burglarized the office of Glover & Seqnin on East Market Street of $40.[199] He met a lover of his, Mrs. James Stellar in Cincinnati afterward. On August 12th, her husband saw her at the Western Union Telegraph office there and notified the police. Linson was arrested and Indianapolis Police notified.[200]

---

[197] *The Indianapolis News* – July 30, 1892, p.1
[198] *The Indianapolis News* – August 9, 1892
[199] *The Indianapolis News* – August 13, 1892, p.7
[200] The Cincinnati Enquirer – August 13, 1892, p.16

On August 28, 1892, three boys aged 12-18, who had come to Indianapolis from Chicago, stole a horse and buggy owned by Henry W. Tutewiler from in front of a church. They drove to the north side of town to try and sell them. One of them went to Tutewiler to inquire about a reward. Police were notified and on the night of August 29th, Detectives Thornton and James arrested George Deney and another boy. The third escaped on a train. Tutewiler declined to prosecute and they were held for loitering.

Word was received by Chief of Detectives Timothy Splan that George Stephenson, one of the most noted horse thieves in the country, had stolen a horse and buggy at Gosport, in Owen County, Indiana and traded it for a sulky (horse drawn buggy)and drove to Indianapolis.

At Downing's stable in Indianapolis Stephenson secured a red wagon to replace the sulky and drove through town. Splan detailed Detectives Thornton and James on this case. When Stephenson saw Thornton he started to run. Ben caught him after a chase. On August 30, 1892, Stephenson was taken to Martinsville to answer a charge of grand larceny.[201]

Maria Selika Williams

Madame Marie Selika[202] appeared at A.M.E. Zion Church on Blackford Street the night of August 30th. She performed two musical pieces. Essie Thornton hosted a

---

[201] *The Indianapolis News* – August 30, 1892, p.5

[202] Marie Selika Williams (c. 1849–1937) was an American coloratura soprano. She was the first Black artist to perform in the White House.

reception at her home on Bright Street the afternoon of August 31st for Madame Selika. Many musical people attended.[203]

---

203 *The Indianapolis News* – August 31, 1892, p.8

CHAPTER 7: "IN OUR BUSINESS THE LEAST LITTLE THING SOMETIMES LEADS TO THE GREATEST RESULTS"

After roll call one day in early September, 1892, Ben Thornton shared his experiences as a detective with a News reporter.

"In our business, the least little thing sometimes leads to the greatest results", remarked Detective Ben Thornton the other day after roll call. I remember how we worked 2 or 3 years ago to capture a gang of thieves who were terrorizing the town. Robbery after robbery occurred and we could get no clew (spelling commonly used through the 1950's for "clue"), and it was anything but encouraging. Men were held up, houses were robbed at the rate of 5 to 8 a day."

"One day I got a 'tip'. I drove 15 miles to secure possession of a pair of 15 cent gloves that had been stolen. The gloves turned out to be a valuable clew which, when followed, resulted in the capture of the Fred Piper gang. The property taken in some twenty-five robberies was recovered, six thieves captured and all of them convicted. Fred Piper, the leader, got 14 years and is now serving his time in the Michigan City prison. Even the receiver of the stolen goods was captured and sent to the State's prison." [204]

The News noted the upcoming 15th wedding anniversary of Ben and Essie Thornton, which occurred October 10, 1892.[205]

On September 27, 1892, Mitchell Winn of 285 West North Street, was stabbed in the back by another man who walked by him at the corner of Indiana Avenue and West Street. The assailant escaped. Police Surgeon Earp tended to the wound, which he pronounced as "serious, but not dangerous."[206] On September 30, 1892, Ben Thornton arrested Frank Stubbs for this assault.[207] Stubbs was tried in Criminal Court on October 24th, convicted of assault

---

[204] *The Indianapolis News* - September 8, 1892, p.5
[205] *The Indianapolis News* – September 26, 1892, p.2
[206] *The Indianapolis News* – September 28, 1892, p.2
[207] *The Indianapolis News* – September 30, 1892, p.2

and sentenced to three months imprisonment in the work-house.[208]

Ben made a trip to Winchester, Virginia to retrieve a prisoner named Thomas Mack, charged with burglary and grand larceny. They returned to Indianapolis the night of October 7, 1892. Mack was bound over to court the next morning.[209]

Days later, Ben talked to the News about the significance of visiting Winchester, which was near the Ohio line:

"Detective Ben Thornton, just returned from Winchester, Randolph County (Indiana), said":

"This is the first time I have been in Winchester for thirty years, but I shall never forget my first and only other visit. I bad hired out to a man in that neighborhood to learn the blacksmith's trade, and not being overburdened with cash I walked the whole distance. All my earthly possessions were in an old-fashioned carpet- sack. It was about 4 o'clock in the afternoon when I got there. The

---

208 *The Indianapolis News* – October 24, 1892, p.2

209 *The Indianapolis News* – October 8, 1892, p.1

man treated me first rate but his wife didn't. 'You can teach him the blacksmith's trade if you want to,' she said to her husband, 'but no nigger can sleep in my house. Let him sleep in the barn.'"

"Of course that was not pleasant, and I sat around and listened to the pair wrangle over me until I got tired, and then, picked up my carpet-sack, started out on foot for Indianapolis. The first night I walked seven miles, and stopped at a farm-house. The old woman living there—bless her heart! I never shall forget her—had two sons in the army, and as I had been a soldier she took mighty good care of me until the next day, when I reached Richmond. I made my way back to Indianapolis by easy stages and gave up all thoughts of learning the blacksmith's trade."[210]

Detectives Thornton and James caught up with Samuel Shears the evening of October 25, 1892. He was wanted at Evansville for horse stealing. Shears spent 1892-1894 in the Indiana State Prison.

---

[210] *The Indianapolis News* – October 15, 1892, p.12

For several days in late November, 1892, complaints had come in of a man insulting women at New York and Illinois Streets in the morning or evening. He would hug and kiss them and let them go. Two uniformed officers were placed there but failed to catch him. On the morning of November 30th, Detectives Thornton and James were stationed there.

Just before 6 a.m., Mrs. Barbara Trott, who kept a boarding house, walked across the street. As she did so a man matching the description of the suspect appeared on the other side of the street and started toward her. Ben accidently showed himself underneath the lamp-post and the suspect did not molest Mrs. Trott. The man was placed under arrest however and identified as Arthur Locklear. He was held for assault and battery.[211]

The defendant, Arthur Locklear, was tried for the assault on Mrs. Trott on December 1st. She could not identify him completely so he was acquitted. As he was leaving the court room, Ben Thornton served

---

[211] *The Indianapolis News* – November 30, 1892, p.2

a warrant on him, charging Locklear with assaulting Mrs. Christina Phillips.[212]

On Saturday morning, December 3rd, Mr. Locklear, of 440 Douglass Street, appeared in police court, accused of assault and battery on Christina Phillips, 154 Bird Street, a restaurant employee. Mrs. Phillips made positive identification. However, a number of people came forward in his defense, speaking of his good character.

Judge Buskirk said to Detective Thornton that he had been told that Thornton had acted as a persecutor of Locklear, to which Ben responded vigorously, insisting that the defendant's attorney, Horace Smith being sworn to show that he (Thornton) had been friendly toward Locklear. Ben said he had acted several times in his behalf. Ben cross-examined Attorney Smith himself and the judge said at last he was satisfied that the detective had not imposed himself upon Mr. Locklear. However, due to Locklear being given an

---

[212] *The Indianapolis News* – December 3, 1892, p.2

alibi for the Phillips assault by witnesses, he was discharged.[213]

On the night of Saturday, December 10, 1892, three men, William Kimble, Harry McCormick and Tom Foree visited Haberern's saloon, 504 North West Street. After it closed, McCormick and Foree asked to come in the back door. The owner refused them and was told that William Kimble was injured. He helped the others take Kimble home. McCormick and Foree said that Kimble had fallen down near the pump and hurt his head. The three men had been drinking.

Ben Thornton was assigned to this case and when he interviewed McCormick, the man admitted that the injury was made by a fall, but after McCormick had struck Kimble. This was due to an insult. He implicated Foree in the assault. Ben arrested both of them about 6 p.m. December 13th, charging them with assault and battery with intent to kill.

Dr. Hodges said on December 14th that Kimble was in critical condition and if he did

---

[213] *The Indianapolis News* – December 3, 1892, p.2

live, he might be permanently injured.[214] In fact, William Kimble did die of his injuries within a few days and McCormick and Foree were held for the grand jury on December 29th on a bond of $5,000 each, for being an accessory to the death.[215] McCormick was still in jail April 29, 1893 when he finally was bailed out of jail. There is no record of the outcome of this case but it does not appear McCormick or Foree served any more time for this incident.

Detective Samuel James left the Indianapolis Police Department and became a member of the Indianapolis Fire Department in 1893. Ben Thornton's partner in early 1893 was Martin McGuff. Martin McGuff (1852-1931) had himself worked for IFD since 1874. He joined IPD as a detective around 1892.

---

[214] *The Indianapolis News* – December 14, 1892, p.2
[215] *The Indianapolis News* – December 29, 1892, p.2

Martin McGuff

Born: February 1852 California, OH.
Died: July 12, 1931 Indianapolis, IN.
April 3, 1874: Hoseman for IFD Hose Co. 7.
December 29, 1883: Foreman of IFD No. 2 Engine Company.
December 20, 1892: Detailed from his job as an IPD
Detective to investigate arson fires from IFD.
1896: IPD Detective.
March 6, 1901: Serving as patrolman with IPD.
July 21, 1914: Fire Lt. Martin McGuff of Engine
House 13 severely injured in a collision of two trolleys.
1927: Retired from IFD, 42 total years of service.

After 18 years with the Indianapolis Fire Department, he changed to the Indianapolis Police Department with a change of administration (1892). He spent 11 years with IPD.
Buried Crown Hill Cemetery.

The office of Dr. Burton, 818 North Illinois Street, was broken into the night of Sunday, August 8, 1893. Clothing and money were taken. Detectives Thornton and McGuff suspected a man named James Carter in this theft and finally became convinced of his guilt.

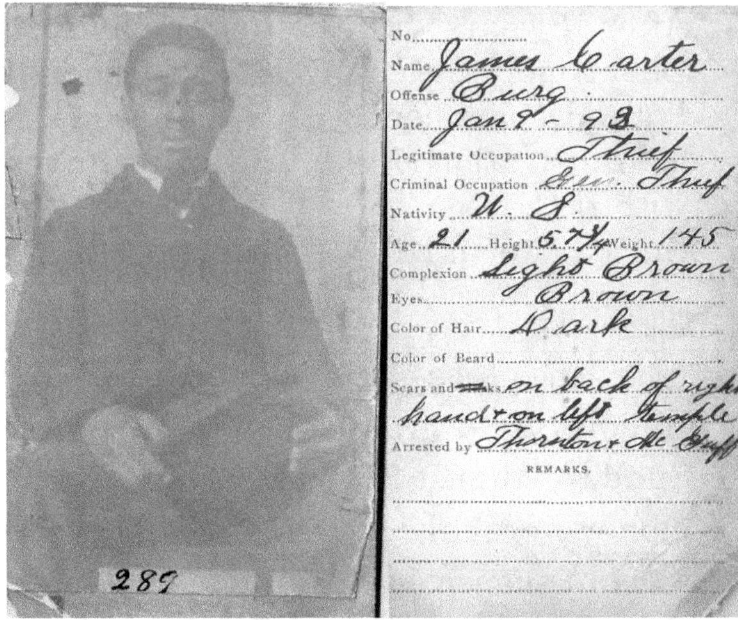

289

No.
Name James Carter
Offense Burg
Date Jan 9 - 93
Legitimate Occupation Thief
Criminal Occupation Gen. Thief
Nativity U. S.
Age 21 Height 5 7 1/4 Weight 145
Complexion Light Brown
Eyes Brown
Color of Hair Dark
Color of Beard
Scars and Marks on back of right hand & on left temple
Arrested by Thornton & McGuff

REMARKS.

[216]

The detectives found and arrested Carter at Heston's saloon on Kentucky Avenue, January 10th and charged him with burglary. He admitted his guilt. Carter also admitted committing the robbery of a mail sack taken from Union Station two weeks earlier and that he had taken the overcoat of Probate Clerk Buskirk from the court house.

He also told them where to find the overcoat stolen from Patrick Gorman, clerk of Mayor Sullivan and one taken from William Moore of the Treasurer's Office.

---

[216] Indianapolis Police Department mugshot.

On the morning of January 11th, Carter was held for the grand jury. Aged 22, he had spent 12 years in the Plainfield reform school. [217] Convicted, Carter spent February 10, 1893 to August 18, 1895 in the Indiana State Prison.

The home of S. Jamison, at Nash and 10th Streets, was burglarized February 10, 1893. A pair of shoes left in the house by the suspect provided a clue. Detective Thornton was assigned to the case. Information came in the morning of February 20th to the Detective department that the suspect was in Gas City, Indiana, where he was known as John F. Clark.

Ben Thornton left immediately for Gas City, saw his quarry and arrested him. He had him back to the depot in time for the return trip to Indianapolis. Clark's real name was said to be Frank Powell, who had served a term in the penitentiary.[218] On March 13, 1893, Judge Cox accepted Powell's plea of guilty to burglary and sentenced him to five years in prison.[219] Powell served a

---

[217] *The Indianapolis News* – January 11, 1893, p.7
[218] *The Indianapolis News* – February 20, 1893, p.1
[219] *The Indianapolis News* – March 13, 1893, p.8

term from March 16, 1893 to December 11, 1896.

Boys Burglary Ring Broken Up

Police had taken burglary complaints for the past 10 days in March, 1893, up and down Hoyt and Lexington Avenues on the southeast side of town. Seven school houses were broken into and various items stolen. Detectives Thornton and McGuff arrested three boys, Dee Smitherman, J. Smitherman and J. Martin, the oldest 10 years old.

When interviewed at police headquarters, Martin admitted that the three, along with some others, burglarized the school houses along with 10 break-ins of private homes.[220]

On April 1st, Detectives Thornton and McGuff made another arrest related to this burglary case. Lyle Justice, 10 years old, was arrested for burglary. Taken to headquarters, he confessed in Chief Splan's office to 17 burglaries, mainly in the Lexington and Hoyt Avenue areas. His method of operation was to go to a house and ask if a certain person was there. If no one

[220] *The Indianapolis News* – March 25, 1893, p.6

was home, he would inform the rest of the "gang" and as Justice was small in size, they would put him through the transom or window and he would open the door for them. The value of recovered property was estimated at $500.[221] McGuff and Thornton arrested Lawrence Olive on April 3rd for his part in the burglary spree. The detectives recovered almost all the stolen property.[222]

[221] *The Indianapolis News* – April 1, 1893, p.7
[222] *The Indianapolis News* – April 3, 1893, p.2

CHARLES E. EYSTER.

Charles Eyster

A senseless crime occurred the night of April 14, 1893 at Third and Mississippi Streets. Charles E. Eyster, 28, the druggist at the pharmacy there was serving two men who came in to make purchases. They bought a deck of playing cards and came back for some cigarettes. A later account said that they exchanged the playing cards for a pair of dice. Eyster's wife was present at this time and then went upstairs. As Eyster was waiting on them, one of them said "You ought to be an angel", drew a pistol and fired, striking the druggist in the abdomen. The two men, described as African-American, fled the scene. Eyster's wife came downstairs at the sound of the shot and her husband fell into her arms. He said "I've been shot." When Mrs. Eyster asked who shot him, he replied that it was "The two negroes who bought the dice."

All through the night, Indianapolis patrolmen Nathan Ward, Daniel Carter and Tobin worked on the case. The officers said that a few nights earlier, they had arrested two African-American "desperate toughs", John Parker and Edward McAfee. Parker tried to use a knife on Ward, who knocked him down. This arrest was made near Eyster's drug store and the men were taken inside to wait for the arrival of the patrol wagon.

Inside the drug store, Parker and McAfee were so loud and disorderly that the clerk insisted they be taken out, which they were. While waiting, the prisoners were loudly threatening Charles Eyster and his clerk. Parker and McAfee were fined the morning of April 14th and after leaving Police Court threatened the officers and said they would "get even" with the druggist and his clerk.

Daniel Carter **Nathan T. Ward**

The above officers investigated the case the night of the shooting and had previously arrested John Parker & Edward McAfee. Before he died, Charles Eyster reportedly told Patrolmen Carter and Ward that a "colored man" had shot him.

Reportedly, Parker and McAfee then visited a saloon near the drug store, again making threats. That night, when screams were heard, inside that saloon, an African-American man said knowingly, "Oh, I know what that is. I guess there are some people who won't send in anymore telephones for the wagon."

The screaming came from Mrs. Eyster, calling for help after her husband was shot. Parker and McAfee, who answered the description of the assailants, were searched for by officers in all their known haunts.

Charles Eyster died of his wounds on the afternoon of April 15th. Detectives Martin McGuff and Benjamin Thornton arrested Parker and McAfee. They took them to Eyster's home for identification, but it was too late, Eyster had died. Both men denied any involvement in the shooting.[223] One of them had a new pair of dice on them when arrested, the News reported on April 21st.[224]

By April 17th, Indianapolis police were still searching for the assailants of what Superintendent Thomas Colbert described as "one of the most cold-blooded, causeless murders that ever came under his notice." John Parker and Edward McAfee were taken before Colbert and Chief of Detectives Timothy Splan. They denied all knowledge of the crime. Parker said he was at the home of a woman named Carrie Spaulding from 8

---

[223] *The Indianapolis News* – April 15, 1893, p.1
[224] *The Indianapolis News* – April 21, 1893, p.2

pm., until the morning after the shooting. McAfee said he went to the express office early in the evening and then joined Parker at the Spaulding house.

Carrie Spaulding and a Miss Bessie King came to police headquarters the night of April 15th to visit the prisoners and had a long talk with them. The women told the same story as to the men's whereabouts. Patrolmen Simpson Hart and Clinger locked the women up for a misdemeanor but that was an effort to get more information out of them.

Rumors of a lynch mob forming to forcibly remove the prisoners from police headquarters began circulating on the 17th and a crowd of about 300 men loitered in the area during the day. In Police Court that morning, the examination of Parker and McAfee was continued.

Detective Thornton said, "This is one of the most peculiar cases that have ever come under my notice. I do not consider the case against Parker and McAfee a strong one. I know them so well that I believe if they had done the shooting they would have left town at once. If they get into a simple fight they leave until everything quiets down. I cannot get a clew to any motive of the crime. I have made a careful examination of Eyster's home relations and they were happy.

His financial condition was good. I thought, perhaps, it might have been a case of suicide, but I can find nothing to base that theory on. I sometimes think the shooting was not done by colored men at all."[225]

The widow of Charles Eyster was brought to the Marion County Jail on April 20, 1893 to look at John Parker and Edward McAfee in order to make identification if possible. She had just recovered from the shock of the murder and sat down in the jailer's private room, while Martin McGuff and Ben Thornton went to retrieve the prisoners.

The prisoners were brought in and stood before Mrs. Eyster. She looked from one man to the other for two full minutes without saying anything. They were taken out of the room and Ben Thornton said "Well, madam, what do you think?" Raising her

---

[225] *The Indianapolis News* – April 17, 1893, p.1

head, covered by a mourning veil, she said in a determined voice, "They are the men." After being given another look at the men, she stated "They are the men who killed my husband." [226]

John Parker and Edward McAfee were indicted for murder in the first degree, May 11, 1893. The evidence was largely circumstantial. This case would become one that would involve Ben Thornton and have a large impact on his career as time went on. At this time, Ben was having serious doubts about the guilt of John Parker and Edward McAfee in the Charles Eyster murder.

Murder Suspects Sought

The same day that Parker and McAfee were indicted, Chief of Detectives Timothy Splan received a dispatch from James Shoecraft, marshal of Yellow Springs, Ohio, telling him to arrest Samuel Craft and George Ross, for the murder of John Valentine.

The message said that Valentine had arrived at Yellow Springs on May 10th and became sick and died shortly afterward.

---

[226] *The Indianapolis News* – April 20, 1893, p.5

Before he died he said he had been in Indianapolis and was robbed and assaulted by the two men named in the cable. About 9 p.m. on May 11th, Detectives Thornton and McGuff arrested the two men and took them to the police headquarters jail.

They admitted being with Valentine and helped him to spend his pension money but denied assaulting him in any way. Craft said that while Valentine was in Indianapolis, he took sick. A letter from the coroner of Yellow Springs stated that Valentine died from a kick in the side supposedly administered by the prisoners.[227]

Charles Eyster Murder Trial Begins

On May 31, 1893, as the trial began in the Charles Eyster murder case, the State introduced Detectives McGuff and Thornton to testify as to the arrest of the defendants. Detective McGuff testified that he arrested Parker on the day after the shooting. He found in his pocket two dice. They were new dice and so marked that he would be able to identify them. He testified that the

---

[227] *The Indianapolis News* – May 12, 1893, p.1

defendants wanted to be taken before Eyster to see if he would identify them. They were prevented from doing so when Eyster's physician said the man was dying and no one could see him.

Coroner Beck testified the bullet removed from the body of Eyster was a .32 slug. He was followed on the stand by Patrolman Nathan T. Ward. He said he arrested McAfee a month before the shooting (not a few days as stated by the News on April 15th). Ward telephoned for the patrol wagon from Eyster's store.

The Wednesday night before the shooting he also arrested Parker and also telephoned for the wagon from Eyster's store. Parker was so violent and obscene in the store that he was taken outside at the request of the clerk, Arthur Layton.

Ward stated that once outside, Parker threatened to kill him (Ward) and his partner, Dan Carter and everybody else who assisted in his arrest. Parker was sent to the work-house but got out the following Friday.

Patrolman Daniel Carter testified to the same facts as Patrolman Ward. He also said that he had seen Parker on Friday night put his head in the doorway of Venable's saloon. This was 30 minutes before the shooting and only a short distance from the scene.[228]

Officers Simpson Hart and Clinger testified as to finding the supposed murder weapon in the home where the arrests were made. The gun had recently been fired they testified. On June 1st, the prosecution began examining witnesses and among those who testified was the widow of Mr. Eyster, who identified the defendants in court as the ones who bought the dice. Drug store clerk Arthur Layton testified that the dice found on John Parker were the type sold at the drug store.[229]

On June 2, 1893, *The Indianapolis News* published a story alongside the latest news of the Eyster trial, which stated Detective Benjamin Thornton was to be asked by police authorities for an explanation concerning his actions in connection with the Parker and McAfee case. It was known that Thornton was never

---

[228] *The Indianapolis News* – May 31, 1893, p.2
[229] *The Indianapolis News* – June 1, 1893, p.2

strongly impressed with the evidence against the two defendants. It was alleged he had not done all he could in procuring evidence in the case.

Ben stated in response that done his whole duty in the case and did not fear any investigation. Superintendent Colbert when asked about the complaints against Thornton, declined to discuss them. He said that Thornton would be asked to make an explanation to the Commissioners of the Board of Safety.

Prosecutor Holtzman stated that Ben Thornton had been trying to discredit all of the State's witnesses before the grand jury and that he made insinuations about the domestic relations of Eyster which were not justifiable.

Ben Thornton said he will be a witness for the defense, "I am a witness to tell the truth as I found it. I and detective McGuff arrested these men. At the time I began on the case I was sincere in the belief that they were the guilty ones. Two hours and a half after they were arrested I went to Mrs. Eyster and she described other persons to me. The only part of her description that fitted Parker and McAfee was that one was darker than the other. The first man on the scene after the shooting was a man named Gabler. He saw a "Negro" run south on Mississippi Street and up the alley, and he says he told Officer Ward of this fact before Ward went into the store. In my investigation of this case I have found enough to satisfy me that the accused are guiltless and whatever my testimony may show will be given. I have been told that to testify in their behalf will be to invite charges to be preferred against me; I have also been told that by doing so I will take my life in my own hands. I am not afraid of charges or dismissal from the force. I have been connected with the police force for 17 years, and my record is honorable and unimpeachable. In this case I have not told the defense a single thing except to express the belief to attorney Kealing the day of the preliminary examination that my testimony would not help the prosecution. An officer came to me and proposed that we say to the two girls in this case that if they would swear that Parker and McAfee were guilty they would be released, and if not, that they would get six months in Police Court. I declined to have anything to do with him. I have never made my cases in that way and do not want to begin now."

The *News* ended their story by saying Thornton has been reading law for several years and says he can practice law with as much success as he has had in the police work.[230]

[230] *The Indianapolis News* – June 2, 1893, p.2

CHAPTER 8: "ONE OF THE MOST EFFICIENT DETECTIVES THE CITY HAS EVER HAD"

On June 3rd, Carrie Spaulding testified. She said John Parker came to her home on Anderson Street between 7:50 and 8 o'clock on the evening of the murder and did not leave it until 10:30 p.m., when he left to get beer along with Edward McAfee, who had just come to the house from the express office.

When he returned he stayed at her home all night. She also testified that officers Dan Carter and Simpson Hart had told her if she did not change her testimony they would send her to the work-house. Bessie King testified to the exact same thing, she being at Spaulding's home during this time.[231]

Trial resumed for the murder case of Charles Eyster, Monday, June 5th in Criminal Court. Detective Thornton was the second witness called by the defense. He testified

---

[231] *The Indianapolis News* – June 3, 1893, p.7

that when he arrested the defendants they asked to be taken before Eyster for identification; that the dice found on McAfee were old ones; that McAfee was dressed in dark clothes and parker in light trousers and brown hat and that the description Mrs. Eyster gave him of the men after they were arrested did not fit the defendants.

Ben also testified that Patrolman Dan Carter wanted him to say to the two female friends of the defendants that if they didn't testify they would be sent to the work-house. The work-house was a prison of sorts for people convicted of petty crimes. The prosecution did not cross-examine Thornton.

Edward McAfee's parents both testified to the fact that he was in their home until about 9 p.m. the night of the murder, when his mother sent him to the express office.

McAfee took the stand and said he knew both the victim Eyster and the clerk Layton well, having lived in the neighborhood for 8 years. On the evening of the shooting he ate supper and stayed at home until nearly 10 o'clock, when he was sent to his mother to the express office with a bundle to be shipped to his brother in Michigan City. He then went to Mississippi and Second streets, waiting for a car. McAfee took a car from Mississippi Street and went to Union Station where he secured a receipt for a package. The receipt was taken away from him by Detective Thornton.

McAfee continued that he went to Carrie Spaulding's house, where he found John Parker, Carrie Spaulding and the Bessie King woman. He stayed there all night. The dice found on him were given to him by George Perseley. He denied going to Eyster's Drug store the night of the murder. The broken revolver was one that he and Parker were playing with at Spaulding's residence.[232]

On June 6th, testimony continued in the Eyster case. George French testified to corroborate what time Edward McAfee came to Carrie Spaulding's home, where French lived. He testified that he went to sleep at 9 p.m. and that when Carrie Spaulding woke him up, McAfee was there.

---

[232] *The Indianapolis News* – June 5, 1893, p.2

John Parker, the co-defendant, denied every accusation against him, telling the same story as McAfee.

Harry Seibert, clerk in the American Express office at the depot, testified that he believed McAfee brought the package for his brother there between 8:30 and 9 o'clock.

Patrolmen Tieben and Patrick and Mr. James Ward testified that the witnesses, Carrie Spaulding were at Ward's saloon on the same night that they claimed they were at home with the defendants.

Ben Thornton was recalled to testify that he had seen Carrie Spaulding and Bessie King with Lee Essick at Ward's saloon on Saturday night (not the night of the murder). Miss Spaulding was recalled and denied she had been at Ward's on Friday night but she had been there on Saturday.[233]

At 4 p.m. on Monday, June 12, 1893, the jury returned from their deliberations in the trial of John Parker and Edward McAfee. The verdict was guilty. The recommendation from the jury was they should suffer death.

---

[233] *The Indianapolis News* – June 6, 1893, p.6

The defendants sat "rigid and horrified". After the verdict, they were taken in charge by Sheriff Emmett and seven deputies and taken to jail. The Marion County Court House was directly north a block away from the Marion County Jail. Along this route, Alabama Street was lined by a curious crowd, asking "What was the verdict?" Parker and McAfee paid no attention to the remarks of the throng.

In the jail, the men were held outside a cage for a few minutes and were surrounded by reporters. As the handcuffs were being removed, a News reporter asked them how they felt, to which Parker replied: "I feel damn bad. I feel that I ain't had justice done. There's justice written on the four sides of the court room but there is no justice for a nigger…they can't hang us. We'll fool them. We'll get a new trial."

At that point McAfee broke in and said, "Why in the devil just don't that jailor put us inside. We don't want to be stared at."[234]

The next day, *The Indianapolis News*papers carried a story that Ben

---

[234] *The Indianapolis News* – June 12, 1893, p.2

Thornton would be brought up on charges of conduct unbecoming an officer for his actions in the Eyster murder case. He was described as “one of the most efficient detectives the city has ever had.”[235]

The Case Against Lon Henderson

Lon Henderson

[235] *The Indianapolis Journal* – June 13, 1893

Late in the afternoon on June 16, 1893, a woman who lived at 612 Cornell Avenue reported that her mule had been stolen a mule from her stable by Alonzo "Lon" Henderson, a known criminal. Detectives Thornton and McGuff were assigned to the case. The woman, later identified as Mary Rafferty, told McGuff and Thornton that Lon Henderson had admitted to her his involvement in the shooting and possible death of a man named John Tarpey in Haughville, June 1st.

Thornton directed her to the police clerk to make her written theft report. Then he turned to McGuff and said, "There is no one here to report this thing to, but I suppose there will be no objections if we go after Henderson without being detailed?"

"I think not", replied McGuff.

The following day at 3 a.m., Merchant policeman Chris Hanson discovered two burglars in the grocery store of Otto Schmidt, at Delaware and McCarty streets. They were emerging from the store when Hanson caught one of them and placed him under arrest.

As Hanson was doing so, the other man stepped up, placed a pistol in Officer Hanson's face and ordered him to throw up his hands. Hanson obeyed. As the two suspects fled, Hanson pulled his pistol and fired, shooting one of the men in the head. The man fell to his knees, but got up again and made his escape. Hanson identified him as Lon Henderson.[236]

On June 17th, Thornton and McGuff went to Henderson's mother's home. They shadowed the home and were rewarded when they saw Lon Henderson sneak in. At noon, the detectives forced their way in and a desperate battle followed with Henderson and his mother.

Henderson was behind the door with a knife in one hand and a pistol in the other. His mother Mary Henderson and sister Mrs. Dora Gillian, struck the officers with clubs on the heads and arms, so Henderson could use his knife. They also threw every object she could grab, wood, furniture and cooking utensils at the police.

---

236 *The Indianapolis News* – June 17, 1893, p.2

They managed to wrest the revolver from Henderson's hand but he held onto the knife. McGuff was knocked to the floor and as he fell, he shot Henderson in the left leg. At that same time, so close together that both reports sounded like one gunshot, Thornton fired, striking Henderson in the right leg. After a 20 minute fight, the detectives captured him.

Over 200 persons gathered around the home while the wagon was on its way from headquarters. With guns drawn in case any of Henderson's friends tried to rescue him, he, his mother and sister were loaded into the patrol wagon. The women were charged with assault and battery with intent to kill, Lon Henderson with burglary and larceny.

Henderson had tried to shoot Chief of Detectives Timothy Splan on February 16, 1890. When examined at the police station he was found to have a third bullet wound, believed received from Merchant policeman Hanson.

Nathan T. Ward

Born: March 1853 Union County, Indiana
Died: March 20, 1908 Indianapolis, Indiana
Date appointed to IPD: May 31, 1878
Date of Separation/Retirement: November 10, 1901
November 10, 1901: Nathan Ward dismissed from force for intoxication.
Buried in Crown Hill Cemetery, plot 37, lot 594.
Nathan T.Ward was 5'11" in height.
March 28, 1908: "Nathan T. Ward, was born at Union County, Ind., 1853 and departed this life Friday morning at the age of 54 years. He served on the Indianapolis Police force for 19 years and for a number of years

held the position of Police Court Bondsman. The funeral services were held Monday afternoon from Bethel Church Rev. Geo. Sampson officiating. He was a member of Pride of the West Ledge No. 2. K. of P."

Charges Filed Against Benjamin Thornton

The morning of June 19th, the Commissioners of Public Safety met. Patrolman Nathan Ward filed charges against Detective Ben Thornton accusing him of conduct unbecoming an officer in trying to assist the defense in the trial of Parker and McAfee. Thornton for his part, also filed a long document in which he denied that he had rendered any assistance to the prisoners.[237]

Meanwhile, on June 19, 1893, Lon Henderson was in City Hospital recovering from being shot by Detectives Benjamin Thornton and Martin McGuff after resisting arrest. His trial for burglary was set back two weeks. He was also implicated in the robbery of the Schmidt grocery.

On the morning of June 20, 1893, a woman named Mary Rafferty gave

---

[237] *The Indianapolis News* – June 19, 1893, p.2

Superintendent Thomas Colbert information that Lon Henderson was the man who shot and killed John Tarpey. The night of the Tarpey murder, Henderson came to her house saying he had shot a man in a Haughville saloon, describing the exact circumstances of the Tarpey murder. He wasn't certain the man was dead or alive. He said before he left that if she ever revealed his story, he would kill Rafferty and her daughter.[238]

The back story on the murder of John Tarpey is as follows. On June 1, 1893, about 1 a.m., four men, including John Tarpey, an iron molder at the Malleable Iron Works, entered a saloon in Haughville. A masked man was behind the bar rifling the cash drawer while the bartender slept on a chair nearby. Tarpey was the last man in the door.

The man at the cash register whirled with a revolver in both hands, firing. Hit twice, Tarpey was killed instantly. The assailant escaped in the confusion. Tarpey was also street commissioner of Haughville. Years later he was referred to as "Marshal"

---

[238] *The Indianapolis News* – June 21, 1893, p.2

of Haughville but he was being confused with Marshal Andrew Dillon of Haughville, murdered June 28, 1890.

Late on June 22nd, while on the operating table, Henderson confessed to police that he murdered John Tarpey but said it was in self-defense.[239]

The Trial of Benjamin Thornton

The evening of Thursday, June 22, 1893, Detective Ben Thornton was given a trial before the Commissioners of Public Safety. He was charged by Patrolman Nathan Ward with conduct unbecoming an officer in the Eyster murder case. It was alleged that while employed as a city detective he worked in the interest of the defendants instead of aiding the State in the prosecution.

When asked by President Hawkins to plead, Thornton pled not guilty. He had a number of witnesses as to his character but they were not heard as the board stated up to this time his reputation as an officer had been good.

[239] *The Indianapolis News* – June 22, 1893, p.9

Patrolman Nathan Ward testified that he filed the charges. After the arrest of McAfee and Parker, he learned that Thornton didn't believe the prisoners guilty. After the identification by Mrs. Eyster of the defendants, Ward asked Thornton what he thought of the case.

He said he did not believe them guilty. Thornton said he had a talk with Chief Splan, who asked why he had made the arrest and he told Splan what he thought of it. A week prior to the prosecution beginning, Thornton asked Ward what was the matter with him. Thornton said, "I don't care a damn how funny you act, I have a right to my opinion."

Ward continued his testimony, stating that Thornton tried to throw discredit on the witnesses, especially Patrolman Dan Carter. He said Dan Carter came to him and said, "Let's go to the girls and have them change their evidence. If they don't, we will send them to the reform school."

Thornton cross-examined Ward on different points during the hearing, but nothing more serious was brought out. Dan

Carter testified that during the trial in Criminal Court while Walden was on the stand, Thornton said to me, "That's the kind of witnesses you've got. He's a darned fool and crazy and his evidence will be thrown out. Why didn't you measure the tracks leading from the drug store?" Carter denied the conversation regarding the King and Spaulding girls.

Thornton testified in his own trial that he had been sent to investigate alleged trouble in the Eyster family by his superior officers.

Testifying in favor of Thornton was William Irwin, Pierce Newton and Judge Cox, as to his ability and that he had never discriminated in doing his duty on account of color. Detective McGuff stated that Thornton had worked as hard on the Eyster case as any other case. McGuff denied some of the statements made by Patrolman Simpson Hart. Mrs. McAfee, mother of Edward McAfee, stated that Thornton had not assisted her son and denounced him for the work he had done against both of her sons, one of which had been put in the State's prison.

Martin Hugg, one of the attorneys for the murderers, declared without reservation that the defense had not received any assistance from Thornton and that the reverse was the truth.

Ben Thornton made a lengthy statement in which he denied he had rendered any assistance to the defense, showed that he had secured some important evidence for the state (finding the dice bought in the drug store before the murder.) He admitted making statements before the grand jury that he did not believe the men guilty and that he did not have much confidence in the State's witnesses.

Thornton stated the Parker and McAfee families were unfriendly to him and he would have no object in trying to befriend them. The board felt in the end, that Thornton had talk too much and was indiscreet in what he said. People unfriendly to him, namely Patrolman Hart, Carter and Ward, had magnified these statements against him.

The board, after an hour of consultation, suspended Thornton for 10 days without pay, gave him a severe reprimand and reduced him to the rank of patrolman. The following morning, June 22nd, he surrendered his badge to Superintendent Colbert. The News stated the general feeling was that the board was too severe in its punishment.[240]

Trial and Punishment of Lon Henderson

In Haughville, crowds gathered on Friday, June 23, 1893, threatening to lynch Lon Henderson. The danger was such that police moved him from his hospital bed to police headquarters. His medical condition was still such that doctors thought he might die of his wounds.[241] On January 13, 1894 in Noblesville, Indiana, Lon Henderson was found guilty of manslaughter in the death of John Tarpey and sentenced to 21 years in prison.

By eating soap, he simulated a mortal case of tuberculosis. The prison physician said he only had 30 days left to live, so Governor Mount pardoned him on September 11, 1899. He would live to shoot and wound IPD Captain Martin Hyland and Merchant

---

[240] *The Indianapolis News* – June 22, 1893, p.8
[241] *The Indianapolis News* – June 23, 1893, p.2

policeman Benjamin A. Bell on March 17, 1902 and commit numerous other crimes before spending over 50 years in the Indiana State Prison.

Thornton is Reinstated

Councilman Puryear started a petition asking for the reinstatement of Ben Thornton to the rank of Detective. It was placed in the hands of Mayor Sullivan, who said he will present it in person to the Board of Public Safety with his signature on it, June 30, 1893.[242]

On the morning of July 3rd, the Board of Public Safety held its monthly meeting behind closed doors. Detective Ben Thornton was reinstated in his old position without much ado. There was a heavy petition from business men asking for this. Thornton had submitted the following letter:

Gentlemen - For seventeen years I have been a member of the police force of the city of Indianapolis, such service has been my life work, and whatever I have done worthy of praise has been done an a police officer. During the investigation of the facts

[242] *The Indianapolis Journal* – June 30, 1893

surrounding the murder of Mr. Charles Eyster I now see I committed some grave indiscretions, but I ask you, gentlemen, to believe that they were indiscretions and not willful wrongs. From the evidence heard by you, gentlemen, you were entirely justified in the judgment you rendered, but In view of my past service, in view of the fact that my past training fits me most exclusively for work in the detective force, and in view of the further fact that my experience in the Eyster case is one I shall never forget, but will ever prevent me from falling into a like error, I most respectfully ask you to modify the judgment you then rendered against me. , Very respectfully,

Benjamin T. Thornton.

This was backed up by a communication from the prosecuting attorney and his assistant asking for a modification of the board's action in reducing him.[243]

In August of 1893, Essie Thornton sold lot 5 and part of lot 4 of Thornton's

---

[243] *The Indianapolis Journal* – July 4, 1893

Subdivision to Benjamin J. Morgan, for $1,575.

On August 19, 1893, A Detective B.D. Haskins of Chattanooga arrived in Indianapolis with a warrant for the arrest of Moses Bush, wanted in Chattanooga for burglary. Detectives Thornton and McGuff were assigned to bring Bush in. They found him in the rear of 418 North East Street. When he caught sight of the detectives, he ran. Thornton overtook him, but Bush shook loose and ran fast away from him.

Thornton fired two warning shots in the air, but Bush refused to stop. A third shot hit the suspect in the leg, bringing him to the ground. The wound was slight and Bush was taken to Chattanooga on August 21st.[244]

---

244 *The Indianapolis News* – August 21, 1893, p.1

An example of the occasional racist opposition Thornton faced comes from an Alton, Illinois newspaper on September 29, 1893.[245]

Ben Thornton, is the name of a very black bogus detective and pension examiner from the city of Washington, Indianapolis or any other place. He has posed as a United States detective in the vicinity of North Alton, and last night arrested a young man charging him with being the Centralia train robber. The young man was delivered to Policeman Swanson who promptly turned him loose. Whether anyone has been taken in by the pension examiner is not known but the authorities are on the lookout for him.

On Saturday night, November 11, 1893, Sam Lee and Hichman Monks got into a fight about a game of craps in Wright's saloon, near the Indiana Avenue canal bridge. Lee left and returned with a revolver in his hand. He then got into a fight with Oscar Franklin, who also was armed. Lee shot Franklin, who

[245] The Alton (Illinois) Evening Telegraph – September 29, 1893

was slightly wounded. Ben Thornton arrested Sam Lee the following morning.[246]

A warrant was sworn out in Police Court, November 23, 1893 for Edward D. Fulford, a foreman of construction of the American Telegraph and Telephone Company. It charged him with forgery along with a William Martland. Ben Thornton, with this warrant in hand, made a fruitless search for Fulford in Greenfield, Indiana and other places. Word came in November 26th that Fulford was arrested in Syracuse, New York.

---

[246] *The Indianapolis News* – November 13, 1893

E. D. FULFORD.

Edward D. Fulford

The following afternoon, Ben left Indianapolis via train for Syracuse, with warrants for Fulford and a requisition for his return signed by Indiana Governor Matthews.[247] Ben Thornton and his prisoner returned to Indianapolis on the afternoon of November 30, 1893.[248]

---

[247] *The Indianapolis News* – November 27, 1893, p.2
[248] *The Indianapolis News* – November 30, 1893, p.2

The Murder of Policeman John L. Watterson

On the night of Saturday, December 23, 1893, Gilman & Carney's meat market, 901 North Mississippi Street (now named Senate Avenue), was broken into. It is believed that Merchant policeman John L. Watterson, African-American, interrupted the burglars.

Watterson had been employed by the Merchant Police for a number of years, patrolling this district. He had a reputation for being attentive to duty. Not long before the burglary, he had chased potential burglars away from this meat market. Early in the week he had warned several of the businessmen that had had reason to believe there was a plot to rob them and warned them to be cautious. This same week, Watterson had come across a clue to a recent safe cracking incident. Two days later he was anonymously warned to "keep out", which made him more determined to investigate.

About 11 p.m. Saturday night, a number of persons in the neighborhood of Gilman & Carney's meat market heard 3 shots fired in rapid succession. C.H. Kaasebaum saw muzzle flashes from the rear of the market. J.O. Briggs, who heard the shots from 126 West 9th Street, saw Officer Watterson run down the alley near his house and disappear. He looked to be chasing someone.

John L. Watterson

John L. Watterson was an assistant brick mason in Indianapolis in the years prior to joining the Merchant Police. About 35, he was described as being very popular, with both white and African-American, known for his magnificent physique and his "dead game" nerve.

Watterson's voice was heard to call "Hey there, help!, help!" and finally shout, "Oh God!, Oh, Minor!" Minor was the name of his police partner. John Schad, a grocer living at 875 North Tennessee Street (now named Capitol Avenue) went after the police after seeing a man lying on the ground across the street. Upon arrival, police found Watterson with a fractured skull and badly stabbed in a vacant lot at 7th Street and Capitol Avenue. Unable to talk, he died within seconds.

Upon investigation, it was discovered that the rear door of the meat market had a panel cut out of it. A small amount of meat and some change was taken. The meat was found near the stable in the rear of the market. Nearby was a cleaver, sticking blade up in the ground, together with the cylinder of the officer's revolver, empty, along with his whistle. There were signs of a struggle and a quantity of blood.

Based on the evidence, the theory of IPD's detectives was that three men broke into the meat market. Watterson came down Mississippi Street from the north, crossed a vacant lot and walked up to the rear of the market and found the burglars emerging. Officer Watterson fired three shots at them, wounding one of them, accounting for the blood on the ground. A struggle ensued. They apparently struck Watterson as he was attempting to reload as two cartridges were found on the ground as if knocked from his hand.

The thieves then ran down the alley, south, across 9th Street. Watterson pursued them, calling for help. A trail of blood led from the back door of the meat market down the alley. The body of John L. Watterson had four "terrible" wounds in the body and a severe gash on the left side of the forehead, 1 & 3/4" long.

He was stabbed once in the heart, once in the pericardium and a third time in the elbow, apparently a defensive wound, the knife breaking off. As his gun was empty, he tried using it as a club, breaking the cylinder, then used his mace, until he was stabbed to death.

At 2:30 a.m. on December 25th, Superintendent Powell and Chief of Detectives Timothy Splan decided to use bloodhounds to track the murderer(s). It was agreed it would be an experiment to track a human being over pavement but it would be worth the trial. A dispatch was sent to W.A. Carter at Seymour, Indiana to bring his bloodhounds at once.

Meeting Mr. Carter at Union Station were Powell and Detectives Kinney and David S. Richards. Outside, waited Chief Splan and Detectives Benjamin Thornton and Martin McGuff. A covered police patrol wagon was sent to take the dogs to the murder scene.

Down through alleys and across streets the dogs led, followed by Detectives Thornton, Kenney and Superintendent Powell behind. By now at least 1,000 people in buggies and on the sidewalk were being kept behind the slowly advancing patrol wagon, for fear they would spoil the scent if they got in front of the dogs.

The dogs hit on different points where blood drops were found on the sidewalk. They found blood in Delaware Street and after finding blood spots near the crime scene, they finally lost the scent. They searched 10 miles between 11 o'clock and 3 p.m. when the search ended.[249]

Although the full resources of the Indianapolis Police Department were brought to bear on the Watterson investigation, clues were few. One possible clue came on December 27, 1893 from Martinsville.

On Sunday morning, the day after the murder, a man had gone to one of Martinsville's citizens. The man was wounded and said he had been in some trouble in Indianapolis and did not want the Martinsville authorities to be aware of his being there. He was furnished with a wagon and taken to a station 20 miles away, where he boarded a train.

IPD detectives were of the opinion that this man was wounded in a saloon fight in Haughville on Saturday night, but Superintendent George W. Powell was going to run down this story. He sent an officer to Martinsville to follow up.[250] Rewards were

249 *The Indianapolis News* – December 25, 1893, p.2

250 *The Indianapolis Journal* – December 28, 1893, p.3

offered in this case, $300 by Superintendent Powell and $100 by the Merchants Police.

John was known as the Highland Place Merchant Policeman. The body of John L. Watterson was buried at 2:30 on December 27, 1893. The casket was taken from his home to the Blackford Street Church. An hour later, it was taken to Crown Hill Cemetery. Hundreds of African-Americans were there as well as many white people. Police Captain James F. Quigley and a platoon of uniformed IPD officers escorted the procession to the cemetery. They were followed by nearly 50 Merchant officers.

On August 2, 1894, an announcement was made by the Indianapolis Police Department that they had arrested one of three men suspected of killing John L. Watterson. The one apprehended was William Cole Sr., about 55 years old. He was found through the work of Patrolmen Joshua Spearis, Simpson Hart and Edward Harris. Harris made out a warrant against William Cole Jr. and John McAfee, the other two suspects who were not in Indianapolis.

Joshua Spearis Simpson Hart

Edward Harris

GEORGE W. POWELL, SUPERINTENDENT OF POLICE.

George W. Powell

Superintendent George W. Powell and the three patrolmen, all African-Americans, were friends of Watterson and still worked on the case. The patrolmen had beats in the area of the murder and were anxious to solve the crime. A break came when several women got into a quarrel. One of them said she could tell something about the killing of Watterson. Patrolman Harris heard of this and got her to tell him all she knew.

The officers found witnesses to show that the night of the murder, the two Coles and McAfee took a wagon out on a foraging expedition. They were seen at the scene of the murder. The next morning the younger Cole and McAfee left Indianapolis and had not been seen since. The warrant was given to Patrolman Hart and Spearis, who went to

Castleton in a buggy after the elder Cole. McAfee was known to be in Chicago. On August 1, 1894, Detective Ben Thornton was sent to get him.[251]

The following day, Ben Thornton returned from Chicago with his prisoner, John McAfee. He arrested him in Evanston.[252] The two were accompanied to Indianapolis by McAfee's attorney, African-American W.W. Johnson.

In court, August 7, 1894, the testimony against William Cole Sr. and McAfee was judged circumstantial and not damaging. Cole was dismissed from court and the Judge indicated he was inclined to do the same with McAfee.

There was one bit of fireworks that occurred regarding Ben Thornton. Thornton was told that Attorney W.W. Johnson had told John McAfee that he, Thornton, had recommended an African-American attorney named Bagley to defend him. This would be against IPD policy regarding officers recommending attorneys.

---

[251] *The Indianapolis News* – August 2, 1894, p.6
[252] *The Indianapolis News* – August 4, 1894, p.1

Thornton was boiling mad at hearing this allegation and said he wanted to wipe up the dusty pavement of Washington Street with the attorney from Chicago.

After the case was over, he went to W.W. Johnson. "I want to see you a minute" he said, walking to him. "Well, I don't want to see you", replied Johnson.

"Well, you will see me!", Thornton exclaimed, grabbing the attorney by the collar and almost jerking him from his feet. "I want to know what you mean by telling such a lie about me. You know that I never said anything of the kind, and you must right me, or I will take it out of your hide."

This matter was brought to Superintendent of Police George W. Powell who investigated it at once. McAfee, when questioned, said Thornton had never said any such statement. Public defender W.V. Rooker, the source of the original allegation, repeated what Johnson had told him and Johnson said he had misunderstood him. Powell exonerated Thornton.[253]

---

[253] *The Indianapolis News* – August 8, 1894, p.1

On August 8, 1903, it was reported that "King of the Ghouls", Rufus Cantrell, infamous as the ringleader of a gang of grave robbers in Indianapolis in the summer of 1902, gave a full confession and affidavit while in Michigan City Prison.

He stated that 8 years earlier, he and two men were playing on the commons of the corner of Capitol Avenue and 17th Street late one night. They noticed two men fighting with a policeman named Watterson. Watterson was overcome, carried to a rear commons area and stabbed two or three times. Cantrell said one of the men was a stone-cutter whose name he gave.

He later met the man who said he had attempted to rob a store, had been discovered by Watterson and murdered the officer in the fight which resulted. The second man in the case lived on Martindale Avenue and in 1903 resided in Philadelphia.[254] Chief of Detectives Captain Samuel Gerber, who investigated the Cantrell gang, put no stock in his testimony, saying he had lied so much we have no confidence in what he says.

---

[254] *The Indianapolis News* – August 8, 1903, p.1

This was essentially the last investigation into the murder of John L. Watterson.

It was stated on March 1, 1894 that during his 17 years as a police officer, Ben Thornton had helped to send nearly 400 criminals to the penitentiary or work-house.[255]

A Case of Racial Justice

John F. Dillon, clerk of the Denison House, had occasion to bodily eject a man who rode the hotel elevator. The man, Charles H. Stewart as African-American and preferred charges of assault and battery. Dillon was arrested on that charge, April 27, 1894.

The trial of Dillon began on the morning of Saturday, April 28th in Police Court. Albert J. Beveridge appeared as attorney for Dillon and J.C. Bagley, African-American, represented Stewart. Beveridge went on to serve as a United States Senator from Indiana from 1899-1911.

---

[255] *The Indianapolis News* – March 1, 1894, p.8

The defense that Attorney Beveridge put forth was that the hotel was responsible for protecting its guests and that the elevator boy was responsible for ascertaining that people riding the elevator had business there. They denied there was any rule forbidding African-American men from using the elevator. The defense also stated that when Dillon asked Stewart where he was going that Stewart replied, "It is none of your damned business" and that Stewart was known about the hotel as a "disagreeable person."

Attorney Bagley introduced evidence to show that the victim Stewart used no profanity, conducted himself well and was assaulted without provocation. He called Detective Ben Thornton to the stand. Thornton testified that three weeks earlier he attempted to ride in the elevator at the Denison and was told by the elevator boy that he could not carry him because of his color. Thornton said that he had watched 500 men taken up in the elevator and had heard no inquiries made of any of them.

Judge Stubbs interjected that he had been in the elevator several times and was asked where he wanted to go by the elevator boy. He intimated that the courts had held that hotels have a right to keep any class of persons from using the elevator if the stairs led to the point where they wanted to go. Anyone not wanting to leave could be ejected, but not without using undue force. The Judge said he would research some points of law for a few days.[256]

When court resumed on Monday, April 30th, Judge Stubbs acquitted John F. Dillon. The Court said there was sufficient controversy in the testimony to raise a reasonable doubt.[257]

Retrial in the Eyster Murder Case

The two defendants on death row in the Charles E. Eyster case, John Parker and Edward McAfee, were given a new trial. It was held in Franklin, Indiana in May 1894. On May 3rd, Detective Ben Thornton was called as a witness for the defense. The night of the murder, Thornton said he went to Parker and McAfee's homes and then to the

---

[256] *The Indianapolis News* – April 28, 1894, p.1
[257] *The Indianapolis News* – April 30, 1894, p.10

home of Carrie Spaulding, where he found them.

While on their way to jail, the defendants asked to be taken before the victim Eyster, saying that he would exculpate them from any connection to the shooting. However, they were denied admission to the house, the physician stating that Eyster was resting and must not be disturbed.

Thornton testified that Superintendent Thomas Colbert instructed him to bring no "colored men" into Mrs. Eyster's presence except the accused and to coach her so that she would be very positive in her identification. Thornton said he argued with Colbert, stating that other African-American people should be brought into her presence, but Colbert would not budge.

During cross-examination, Prosecutor William Holtzman asked Thornton, "Did you not testify for the State in the former trial?"

"Yes, sir."

"I will ask you if you were not suspended twenty days from the police force for your action in behalf of defendants?"

"Yes, sir; at your suggestion."

"I will also ask if it is true or false that you were suspended also because you endeavored to damage the good name of Mrs. Eyster?"

"No sir", replied Thornton, looking Holtzman directly in the face. "And, while I am here" he continued, "I want everyone in the court-room, and every citizen of Indianapolis, to know that I never uttered an unkind word against Mrs. Eyster in any manner. I regard her as a perfect lady."

The court-room burst into much applause at Thornton's reply and as he walked away from the stand, the general opinion of the crowd was that he had gotten the best of the prosecutor.[258] On May 10th, after being out all night and most of the day, the jury returned with a verdict: guilty of murder and a sentence of life imprisonment.

---

[258] *The Indianapolis News* – May 3, 1894, p.6

From *The Indianapolis News* – May 10, 1894

John Parker died on September 17, 1894 of “dropsy”, aged 24.[259] Sick and nearly dead with consumption (now known as tuberculosis), Edward McAfee was paroled by Governor Mount in 1899, after receiving a petition signed by friends and prison authorities. He moved back with his mother, in the rear of the drug store where the crime occurred which he was convicted of. He died there, October 11, 1899.[260]

In response to the court decision over the ejection of C.H. Stewart from the Denison House elevator, 500 African-Americans, mostly men, met the evening of May 7, 1894 to discuss this case and to formulate an appropriate response.

A list of about 50 vice-presidents was read by chairman Gabriel Jones, many prominent persons in the African-American community being named. One of these was Ben Thornton. He arose and declined to serve as a vice-president, saying that there seemed to be an inclination to distribute honorary titles in the emergency.

---

[259] *The Indianapolis News* – September 18, 1894, p.1

[260] *The Indianapolis News* – October 11, 1899, p.17

"What we want", he said, "is not so much empty honor but action in resending such an outrage as has been put upon us. I am not after sympathy or coddling, but my rights and money."

Resolutions were adopted which stated that "we condemn the authorities of the Denison Hotel and demand the prosecution and punishment of the offenders for their inexcusable and insolent violation of the law."[261]

Thornton Frees an Innocent Man

In late March 1894, John Peters, African-American, was accused of stealing the watch of J.D. Brown, while he was working at 131 West North Street. He said Peters took the watch from his vest pocket. He reported the theft to police, who learned that a man with a description matching Peters' was near the North Street address the day of the theft.

Detective Thornton was ordered to arrest Peters, but refused to do so without a warrant. Brown swore out the warrant on

---

261 *The Indianapolis News* – May 8, 1894, p.2

March 19th and Peters was arrested and convicted. He was sent to the work house.

On May 10th, Detective Thornton was investigating a man named Lee Coats of 27 Lafayette Street. While searching the house he found a watch, the style of which was familiar to him. The watch had a serial number of 494,750, which Ben remembered was the number that J.D. Brown gave for his watch. Coats was arrested and Judge Cox freed Peters immediately.[262]

Two Indianapolis men, Moses Anderson and G.W. Benington were arrested in the town of Alexandria for grand larceny on May 11, 1894. Indianapolis police also had a charge of larceny pending against Anderson. Ben was sent on May 12th to Alexandria to retrieve both men. Alexandria was some distance northeast of town.[263]

George Hood, a burglar with a record, was arrested the night of June 15, 1894 by Detectives Thornton, McGuff and P.J. Dougherty after a struggle. He pled guilty to burglarizing the home of Timothy McCarty,

---

262 *The Indianapolis Journal* – May 11, 1894

263 *The Indianapolis News* – May 12, 1894, p.1

174 Massachusetts Avenue.[264] Hood was sent to the State Reformatory from July 18, 1894 to April 12, 1897.

On the evening of June 15, 1894, Ben and Essie Thornton gave a reception at their home to the Thornton Guards. This militia company, designated as M, is part of the Third Regiment of the Indiana State Militia and had existed 11 years at this point. Ben welcomed the company to his house with a short speech.[265]

For several days in July 1894, police had been looking for a man who came to a woman's house, showed her a badge and said he was the partner of Ben Thornton. He had to arrest her for abusing her daughters. She was frightened. The man said the affair could be settled without going into the courts. She refused and resisted him. Ben Thornton caught the man on July 28, 1894. His name was Herbert Wilkinson.[266]

The Indiana delegates to the Knights of Pythias convention at Odd Fellows Hall on

---

[264] *The Indianapolis News* – June 15, 1894, p.2
[265] *The Indianapolis Journal* – June 16, 1894, p.8
[266] *The Indianapolis News* – July 28, 1894, p.6

Indiana Avenue, August 22, 1894 formed a grand State lodge. Ben Thornton was chosen Grand Master of Exchequer for this new organization.[267]

[267] *The Indianapolis News* – August 23, 1894, p.6

Previous Page Illustration

"In All His Glory"

Sketch of an unidentified African-American policeman drawn in 1894 by J. Andre Castaigne for "The Century". It could well have been made with Benjamin Thornton as its model but there is no evidence it was.[268]

[268] By J. Andre Castaigne – "Washington as a Spectacle", August 1894, The Century Magazine, p.491

CHAPTER 9: "I'M GOING TO HAVE MY RIGHTS"

What would develop into a major school segregation case started on September 10, 1894. Essie Thornton took their six year old daughter Addie to School No. 4. She was told the child must be taken to School No. 24, where she was told there was no room for her.[269]

School No. 24 was for African-American children only, while School No. 4 was for white children and black children. Addie went to school at School No. 4 for the next two weeks, until September 23rd, when School Superintendent David K. Goss passed down an order that all African-American children in School No. 4 would have to start attending the "colored" School No. 24 the following day.

On the morning of September 24th, Benjamin Thornton and wife Essie brought Addie back to School No. 4, located at

[269] *The Indianapolis News* – September 11, 1894, p.5

Michigan and Blackford Streets. After accompanying her to the 1B grade in room No. 6, he said to Addie, "Now, there's your seat! You take it and keep it until I tell you to leave."

"There's my child and there she's going to stay", said Ben to the teacher. He then instructed his wife not to remove Addie and left. He was angry. Essie Thornton remained and sat with her daughter for a long time, awaiting her husband's return.

The teacher, Miss Elizabeth Heber, began her instructions to the children, while Essie sat in a chair to one side, keeping an eye on Addie. Addie Thornton was the only African-American in the room. According to instructions issued the day before by School Superintendent David K. Goss, Addie was to be treated as a visitor to the school, not as a pupil.

The previous night, an informal meeting of African-American men was held in the Odd Fellows Hall on Indiana Avenue. The action of Superintendent Goss was discussed and it was decided that he was drawing a color line.

The Indianapolis News interviewed Miss M.S. Ingersoll, principal of School No. 4, who denied the color line has anything to do with the action of Mr. Goss. There were some African-American children in School No. 4 she said, in the 8 AB grade, because that grade does not exist in the "colored school." Further, she said in the 1B grade that Addie was in, it was not fair to white children to be turned away to make room for "colored" children, who can just as well go to School No. 24.

John T. Smith, principal at No. 24, the colored school, said there was a lack of room. The 1AB grade was full. He said many African-American parents had spoken to him about the difficulty in School No. 4.

Addie Thornton stayed in School No. 4 all morning. The teacher said she was instructed to treat her with courtesy and kindness but to treat her as a guest or visitor rather than a pupil.

For his part, Ben Thornton was quoted as follows:

"I am a tax-payer and an American citizen, and I'm going to have my rights. My child is as good as any man's child, and I intend to see that she gets the same treatment as the other children. There's a lot of white people that have just come to this country and think they've got more rights than an American citizen, just because his skin happens to be black. My child is in the school and she is going to stay there. I've already given orders to have a complaint filed and I'll see whether or not there is justice to be had in the courts. I'm not trying to do anything unlawful. It's merely a question of distance. If the colored school was nearest my house I would send my child to it, but the white school's nearest. It's no more just to make my child give up her place to a white child than it would be to ask one of the white children to get out to make room for mine. Besides that, children can't get any kind of education at the colored schools. The teachers don't know anything. The principal of the colored school hasn't got as good an education as I have."

Superintendent Goss said, "I ordered all the colored children out of the lower grades in No. 4 school and told them to go to No. 24, where there is plenty of room. All of the children that were in the lower grades in No. 4 went this morning to No. 24, with the exception of Thornton's child, who was brought here by her parents. Thornton said to me that he would not allow anyone to take his child out of that school. The child stayed there, contrary to my orders. I did not intend to let it stay. Unless there is an order of the court to the contrary, that child will have to go tomorrow.[270]

Superintendent Goss went before the Board of Public Safety and gave notice that he was going to enforce the regulations of the schools and that the board must be responsible if one of their employees, or anybody else, violated the peace.

Superintendent Goss was present at School No. 4 the next day, September 26th when Ben Thornton brought his girl. "I hear you are afraid of me", Ben said to Mr. Goss, "and went to the board."

Goss replied, "Not afraid of you, Thornton, but just taking the precautions to see that the rules were enforced in the vent of your attempting to carry out your threats.

---

[270] *The Indianapolis News* – September 25, 1894, p.10

In the end, Ben accepted the situation for now, saying "Everything is settled, and there is no row, either. There was no use for any policeman. There was merely a misunderstanding in the matter, and Mr. Goss and I have settled everything, and I told Mrs. Thornton to take the child home. I am to see Mr. Goss sometime in the future and the whole difficulty will be arranged."[271]

This case would end up in the courts and it would not be settled for a long time.

The following morning, Thursday, September 27th, Ben Thornton filed suit before Acting Judge Wishard in room 1 of Superior Court. The suit asked for a writ of mandate to compel Superintendent Goss, Supervising Principal Selma Ingersoll and the teacher of the room, Miss Elizabeth Heber, to admit the child to the school No. 4 and teach her.

Judge Wishard issued an alternative write returnable Saturday morning. Thornton insisted that the whole affair is discrimination as to color. Thornton's attorneys were Kealing and Hugg. Their suit

---

[271] *The Indianapolis News* – September 26, 1894, p.8

stated that School No. 4 is a mixed school, that the petitioner is a freeholder and a house-holder and lives within one block of the school and that there is no other school within a distance of four blocks.

It was alleged that Adelaide Thornton was admitted as a pupil on September 10th and had been a pupil ever since in Miss Heber's room. The suit alleged that Goss' claim that the school is crowded is false, that he is acting maliciously and without due regard to the duties owing to Addie E. Thornton and that is solely because she is of negro parentage.

Ben Thornton said that he thought the affair could be amicably settled yesterday, but he couldn't agree to the transfer of his child. He had personal family reasons why she should not be sent to School No. 24. That day, Mrs. Thornton again brought Addie to School No. 4. Principal Ingersoll sent a note to David K. Goss, who was ill at the English Hotel. He sent a note back stating that he would bring legal proceedings against Thornton at once.[272]

---

272 *The Indianapolis News* – September 27, 1894, p.2

This situation became national news, the following story being carried in numerous newspapers:

Fighting Against Class Discrimination.

INDIANAPOLIS, Sept. 28.—An important suit was filed in the superior court here yesterday which may furnish an important precedent. It is by Benjamin Thornton, a prominent colored citizen, who asks a mandate compelling the public school superintendent and his subordinates to admit his child to the public school No. 4. Thornton charges that the child was transferred from this building because it was not attended by colored pupils. Judge Wishard issued an alternative writ returnable tomorrow.

Tyrone (PA) Daily Herald, 28 Sep 1894, Fri, Page 1

On Monday, October 1st, Ben and Essie Thornton withdrew their daughter from School No. 4. Essie explained that they had decided to keep her out of school until the questions presented in court had been settled there.[273]

Ben Thornton's mandamus suit was heard before Judge Winters the afternoon of

---

[273] *The Indianapolis News* – October 1, 1894, p.5

Thursday, October 11, 1894.[274] When asked when he would make a decision in the case on October 25th, Judge Winters deferred, saying he would not make a decision until after the November election. This case would see repeated continuances.[275]

Infanticide Case

A woman named Nettie Cleggett, alias Nettie Henry, was arrested by Ben Thornton for murdering her infant child, on January 14, 1895. The story that unfolded was that she had left her husband at Hartford, Connecticut three years earlier, with a George A. Henry. They had lived in cities such as Philadelphia, Buffalo and Cleveland before coming to Indianapolis.

Nettie gave birth to a baby on December 29, 1894 at 21 Roanoke Street. The infant died 24 hours later. On January 14th, after having an argument with their landlord, a Mrs. Moll Oglesby, Oglesby notified Detective Thornton that the mother had smothered the baby.

---

[274] *The Indianapolis News* – October 11, 1894, p.5
[275] *The Indianapolis News* – October 25, 1894, p.6

Nellie Cleggett was described as aged 22, and coming from a well to do African-American family in Hartford, she herself being slender and delicate of build, wearing glasses. The mother confessed she held her hand over the child's mouth and killed it.[276]

Nettie Cleggett was sent to the woman's prison in July of 1895, where in March of 1896, she gave birth to another baby.[277]

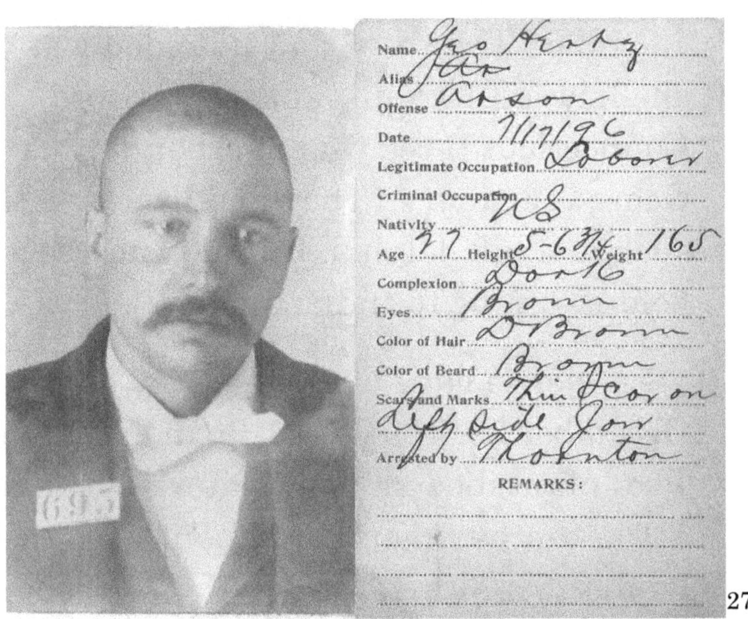

Name Geo Hertz
Alias [illegible]
Offense Arson
Date 1/17/96
Legitimate Occupation Laborer
Criminal Occupation
Nativity US
Age 27 Height 5-6 3/4 Weight 165
Complexion Dark
Eyes Brown
Color of Hair D Brown
Color of Beard Brown
Scars and Marks Thin Scar on Left Side Jaw
Arrested by Thornton
REMARKS:

[278]

A side issue arose from this case on January 26th. Her companion, Mr. George

[276] *The Indianapolis News* – January 14, 1 895, p.2
[277] *The Indianapolis News* – March 14, 1 896, p.7
[278] Indianapolis Police Department mugshot.

Henry, charged with complicity in the infanticide case, came into court and charged Ben Thornton with assault and battery. Thornton said to the judge, "I plead guilty, but I'd like to make an explanation." "All right, go ahead", said the judge.

"Yesterday, when Henry was being taken back, I started through the corridor and he called me. I went to see him, and he said 'What did you want to say that about me for?'

Thornton continued, "I told him that I did not want to argue with him and he said that I had 'sworn to a damned lie.' I hit him once. That's all."

When asked, Thornton said that yes, Mr. Henry was a prisoner in charge of the officers at that time of the assault. While the defense vigorously requested that Thornton be jailed, the judge replied that he would decide in a few days what to do about it.[279]

On January 28th, Judge Stubbs announced his ruling in the case of Detective Thornton. He charged him with assault and battery upon the prisoner George Henry and

---

279 *The Indianapolis News* – January 6, 1895, p.2

fined him $100 and costs, then set aside the penalty.[280]

Benjamin Thornton caught sight of two wanted men, Louis Bainey and Van Tassel, January 28, 1895 on Virginia Avenue. They recognized him however, and made their escape. The following day, detectives Martin McGuff, P.J. Dougherty and Ben Thornton made a search of the south side of town for the men, who were the last of a group of highwaymen who had been active in Indianapolis in years past.

While passing a saloon at 100 South East Street, Detective Doughtery stepped inside and saw two men playing cards. Before he recognized them, Bainey reached for his revolver. Doutherty didn't have time to reach for his, but knocked Bainey down with his fist. He did this twice more before Bainey submitted.

They were under indictment for their part in a series of robberies in November. The rest of the gang had been sent to prison.[281] [282]

---

[280] *The Indianapolis News* – January 28, 1895, p.10

[281] *The Indianapolis News* – January 29, 1895, p.5

On March 24, 1895, the following ladies founded an organization called the Daughters of Charity: Mary Locklear, Victoria Broyles, Emma Floyd, Essie Thornton and Nellie Allen, who served as its first president. This group worked through their church, the Bethel A.M.E. Church. One of the leading African-American charitable organizations in Indianapolis, it celebrated its 32nd anniversary, 1927.[283]

On the morning of March 26, 1895, Detectives Ben Thornton and Jerry Kinney went to the home of Mr. C.S. Hildebrand on North Capitol Avenue. The detectives had been informed and believed it to be true, that a man had come to Hildebrand's home offering to sell jewelry, which matched the description of some jewelry they had been looking for.

The detectives departed after talking to Mr. Hildebrand. That afternoon, while they were in the detective office, Mr. Hildebrand entered. He was indignant and started to complain to Chief of Detectives Timothy Splan of the detective's actions. He said, "The

[282] The Indianapolis Journal – January 30, 1895, p.7
[283283] The Indianapolis Recorder – April 2, 1927

next time you send an officer to my house for information I ask that you do not send that nigger," pointing to Thornton.

Thornton rose from his chair and maintained a defiant attitude. Mr. Hildebrand continued, "He insulted my wife and talked in an ungentlemanly manner."

"That is not true," said Thornton, advancing. "Thornton did not insult your wife, and he talked in a very quiet way," said Kinney. "If you say so," said Mr. Hildebrand, addressing Kinney, "it may be so, but I can't believe that man."

These words were hardly from Mr. Hildebrand's lips when Thornton had him by the collar. Chief Splan jumped up, and Superintendent Powell, who had heard the loud talking, entered, and a cooler second thought came to Thornton, for he let go his hold with the remark: "I won't bother myself with you."

Mr. Powell promised to give the actions of the detectives at the house investigation, but he expressed the opinion that from what he had heard and seen Mr. Hildebrand had done much to aggravate Thornton at the office. He said any complaints there might be should be filed with the Board of Safety.[284]

Foot Chase of a Burglar

Early on the morning of May 22, 1895, citizens in the neighborhood of North Pennsylvania Street and East Michigan Street awoke to the sound of gunfire from multiple revolvers and the yelling of men. Indianapolis Police detectives were chasing a man who they suspected of being a serial burglar.

They had been out patrolling for the man that had climbed into the second floors of residences and carrying off property for two months without being caught. Two nights earlier, a robbery had gotten the entire force engaged in the pursuit.

Ben Thornton was on Pennsylvania Street south of Michigan Street when he observed a man in front of him. He followed the man until he got to Delaware and Vermont Streets, where he turned west, when the man changed direction and came back.

---

[284] *The Indianapolis Journal* – March 27, 1895

Thornton thought this suspicious and yelled at him to stop. He ran down an alley, with Ben following him. Ben fired four times into the air and the man kept running.

Thornton kept chasing him until he caught up to the man at Michigan and Susquehanna Streets. Pointing his revolver at the man's face, he ordered him to throw up his hands. Instead the man took a fighting stance. He broke loose and began running again.

By now, Detectives Martin McGuff and Thomas Stout had arrived, hearing the shots and after seeing the man break away, also began firing. The three detectives caught the man at Pennsylvania and North Streets. The man captured was identified as Clarence Jackson, who had just finished a term in the penitentiary for theft. He was charged with loitering. The detectives were satisfied he was not the second story man however.[285]

Mrs. Thomas Taggart, whose husband had become Mayor of Indianapolis on January 1st of that year, left her bedroom at 4 a.m. on the morning of May 30, 1895, to see

---

[285] *The Indianapolis News* – May 22, 1895, p.7

how her children were doing. They lived at the corner of St. Clair Street and North Capitol Avenue. She found them sleeping, but decided to raise a window since it was too warm. When entering her bedroom, she found a man standing near the window. In his hand was her gold watch.

"Drop that watch, you wretch", she cried. His back was to her and when he heard her voice, he dove out the window. Going out head first, he rolled over to the edge of the porch, caught it with his hands and dropped to the ground. Mrs. Taggart's scream woke her husband and he ran onto the roof of the porch. Within a minute or two, the Mayor heard one shot, then another. This was from the police, who swarmed the area but lost the thief.

Mrs. Taggart described him as a short, well-set, little light skinned African-American male. After he left the house, Patrolman Grannan spotted him and fired from 50 feet away, five times, missing him.[286]

Later that afternoon, the suspect pawned the watch in Cincinnati. He was a

---

[286] *The Indianapolis News* – May 30, 1895, p.2

man who fit the victim's description, small, light skinned man, about 140 pounds. He was arrested later at the race track at Latonia. He gave his name as William Walker and refused to talk and wouldn't come back to Indianapolis without extradition papers.

Indianapolis detectives were convinced this was their second story man. They had notified all local pawn shops to be looking for the loot from his home burglaries and so far, not one item had shown up. Another watch that was stolen a week earlier had shown up in Cincinnati, leading them to believe that was where the thief was selling his stolen goods. Ben Thornton was in Cincinnati on May 25th, searching for stolen property. A list of the missing property was sent to the Cincinnati police.

Word came back the morning of May 29th that a number of gold watches and other jewelry that had been stolen in Indianapolis, had been found in the pawn shops of Cincinnati. They had been pawned May 27th. Detectives noticed a pattern in the burglaries. They took place every third night and it was supposed the thief was spending the intervening days in Cincinnati.

The morning after the theft of the watch, May 29th, Captain James Quigley and Jean Harris went to Cincinnati to watch for the thief. They had the number of the watch and it was given to every pawn shop in town. A detective Allen received a call there from a pawn shop that had the Taggart's watch. It had been pawned by a man matching the suspect's description. Quigley visited the places a man like that would likely go and he found him in due course, at 5 p.m., betting at the Latonia race track.

Ben Thornton filed a warrant the morning of May 30th for William Walker. He left for Cincinnati that day.[287]

Ben Apprehends the "Porch Climber"

On the evening of June 4th, Ben Thornton returned from Cincinnati, with Charles Carr, alias William Walker, in custody. Carr was being charged by the Indianapolis Police Department as being the "porch-climber", suspected of being guilty of numerous burglaries in the city. He

[287] *The Indianapolis News* – May 30, 1895, p.2

specialized in striking some of the best homes in Indianapolis. The police said he was the finest house worker that was ever in the city.

CHARLES CARR, SAID TO BE "THE PORCH-CLIMBER."

Charles Carr, age 28, was born at Danville, Kentucky. He had no criminal record before his arrest this week. The morning of June 5th, he was brought before Chief of Detectives Splan. Detective

Thornton lowered the windows in the room. He looked at Carr, who laughed, realizing what Thornton was up to. He was coy in the interview, saying little. Police felt he had started in April of 1895.

Ben Thornton wrote to Detective Allen of the Cincinnati police, who was also an African-American. He described the stolen articles. This was done each time a burglary occurred and Detective Allen spent much time working on these cases.

Ben brought back from Cincinnati seven watches and a diamond ring recovered there. Total value was over $800. At noon, Chief Splan and Ben tried to interview Carr again. He smiled at them and calmly told them he had never been in Indianapolis before. Police had evidence they were convinced would convict him of over a dozen cases but they suspected as many as 24.[288]

Justice was swift in 1895 and on June 12, 1895, a jury found Charles Carr, the "porch climber", guilty of the burglary of the home of Richard W. Carter. He was

---

[288] *The Indianapolis News* – June 5, 1895, p.2

sentenced to six years in the penitentiary.[289] Carr confessed to all the porch climbing burglaries finally to Thornton. He told detectives where they could find all the pawned goods and Ben went to Cincinnati to redeem them.[290]

Murder in Archie Greathouse' Saloon

Some men were playing craps at the saloon of Archie Greathouse, 10 Indiana Avenue on the evening of June 17, 1895. In the rear of the saloon, the game had gone on for an hour. Frank Taylor had lost all his money, about $2. As the game broke up, Taylor thought he had been cheated. A friend of his told him that the dice were loaded.

Frank Taylor told the man he thought had cheated him, Harry Williams, out of the saloon and asked for his money back. Williams refused and laughed at Taylor. Taylor left the saloon, in search of a revolver. After visiting four or five friends, he finally got one and returned to the saloon. Spotting

---

[289] *The Indianapolis News* – June 13, 1895, p.8

[290] *The Indianapolis News* – June 15, 1895, p.7

Williams he said, "Give me back that $2 you ----- or I'll kill you."

Williams ducked and Taylor fired at him. Williams fell to the ground, while Taylor ran out, pointing his gun at anyone who tried to stop him. The bullet struck Williams in the head, fracturing his skull. Taken to the City Dispensary, the bullet was removed. Harry Williams died at 4:30 a.m. June 18th, without regaining consciousness.

Police detectives were on the case, searching his usual haunts and all trains were monitored leaving the city.[291]

Ben Thornton found Henry Jones in New Albany, Indiana on June 21st in the morning and charged him with killing Harry Williams. During the train ride to Indianapolis, (as related by Ben during the trial on November 4th) the two men spoke about the murder. He said that Henry Jones detailed how the whole incident started. Ben took a revolver from Jones from Jones when he arrested him in New Albany.[292]

---

[291] *The Indianapolis News* – June 18, 1895, p.2

[292] *The Indianapolis News* – November 5, 1895, p.6

They arrived by train at Union Station the morning of June 22nd. Jones was taken to police headquarters and then to police court, where he waived examination by a judge. A charge of first degree murder was placed on him. Afterward, he gave a full confession in detective headquarters.

HENRY JONES AS HE APPEARED IN JAIL TO-DAY.

The story that Henry Jones gave was as follows. "My right name is Henry Jones. I am 25 years old. I was known here by some of the boys as Henry Taylor. I came here about two years ago." He said on Monday evening (June 17th) he was shooting craps on Indiana Avenue in the alley back of Archie Greathouse' saloon. He lost $2. He claimed that he shot for $2 and won, after which Harry Williams grabbed him and took his $4 away and wouldn't return it, laughing. Williams had a gun Jones said.

Regarding the actual shooting, Jones said "I did not want to shoot anybody; I just wanted my money back. I went back to the saloon and as soon as I got in Williams saw me and reached his hand around to his hip pocket. I knew he had a gun and I said, 'Don't you pull that on me.' Then he grabbed me and I pulled out the gun and shot. I saw him fall to the floor and I ran away."

He described his flight, meeting up with a Will Jones (no relation), who joined him on a long walk which ended up on the Monon Railroad in the country, where they hopped a freight train which took him to Monon, Indiana. They went to sleep and when Henry Jones awoke, Will Jones had left. He took another train to Lafayette,

Indiana and finally to New Albany, Indiana. After getting off the train, he was arrested. He had the gun on him. Jones said it was self-defense and he would not plead guilty to murder.

Police detective Jerry Kinney was tipped where to find Henry Jones by Will Jones. He returned to Indianapolis when Henry Jones fell asleep, having become afraid of him. He saw Jerry Kinney on the street and told him what he knew. Telegrams were sent and Ben Thornton picked him up.[293]

The trial of Henry Jones lasted for over a week and on November 7, 1895, he jury found him guilty of murder and sentenced him to 21 years in prison.[294] During the trial, one of the chief witnesses against him as an Omar Thomas, a burglar.

While in jail, Henry Jones threatened several times to kill Omar Thomas in retaliation for testifying against him. On July 5, 1896, Jones stabbed Thomas in the stomach, killing him. He was tried and

---

[293] *The Indianapolis News* – June 22, 1895, p.1

[294] *The Indianapolis News* – November 8, 1895, p.7

sentenced to death. This was the fourth man he was thought to have murdered. On May 6, 1897, Henry Jones was hanged at Michigan City, Indiana.[295]

On June 29th, James Lowderbach, 134 North Pennsylvania Street, was shot in the left side of the neck, from behind, about 8 p.m. The assailant was Fielding Shears. Lowderbach was not seriously injured and was recovering at City Hospital. The two men had been friends for years. Shears, who works at the stock yards, was found there getting off a car by Detective Thornton.

Lowderbach, who recognized Thornton, pulled his revolver. Ben saw it and said "Say, my friend can you tell me where Guyer Street is? I'm kinder lost out here." Suspicions allayed, Lowderbach allowed Ben to get closer to him. Ben jumped, grabbed his pistol hand and cuffed him.[296]

---

[295] *The Indianapolis News* – May 7, 1897, p.1
[296] *The Indianapolis News* – July 1, 1895, p.2

10687, Interior of Negro Building, Atlanta Exposition.

Essie, Ben Thornton's wife, was busy the first week of July 1895. She was one of 11 African-Americans from Indiana appointed commissioners to represent the State of Indiana at an upcoming Cotton States and International Exposition in Atlanta, Georgia. It was their duty to gather exhibits that would show the progress and work of the "negro" in Indiana.[297] These were displayed in the "Negro Building between September 18 and December 31, 1895."[298]

A Serial Killer Strikes in Indianapolis

A 3-year old girl named Ida Gebhard walked out of her home in the west part of Indianapolis on July 18, 1895. She lived at 12 Woodburn Avenue. Her mother noticed her missing shortly afterward but could not find Ida after searching up and down the neighborhood streets.

A massive search was made for her. The evening of July 28th, her body, which was mutilated and sexually assaulted, was discovered. It was located in a box in the stable, the rear of 137 and 139 River Avenue.

The condition of the body indicated her teeth had been knocked out, possibly by a hammer. A bloody hatchet was found sticking in the ground in the stable, with blonde hairs sticking to it. Early suspicions fell on John R. Linson, an uncle of the Silver family that owned the stable. He was a

---

297 *The Indianapolis Journal* – July 6, 1895, p.8

railroad engineer. He had a reputation of being mentally ill. After the police learned of his being seen in the vicinity of the stable on the day of the disappearance, police arrested him July 24th.

The coroner's examination of the body revealed that she had been murdered, a large gash being made in the body either by a sharp, long knife or a blow from a hatchet.

IDA GEBHARD.

WHERE THE BODY WAS FOUND.

On the day Ida's body was found, IPD assigned Chief of Detectives Timothy Splan and Detective Ben Thornton to the case. This murder investigation had excited the people of Indianapolis to frenzy and the usual threats of lynch mob activity were made.

On July 27th, Ben located a sister of Mr. Gebhardt, a domestic at 937 North Meridian Street. Interviewing her, she said she knew of no one there who might have a motive to commit such a terrible crime.[299]

By the 29th of July, police had received a letter from a minister of Champaign, Illinois stating that Linson, the original suspect in jail, was in Champaign, Friday, July 19th, the same date several witnesses said they saw him in west Indianapolis. The minister gave him a quarter and helped him in other ways.

Detectives Splan and Thornton said on the afternoon of July 29th that the results of their investigation are not very satisfactory to themselves so far. They found nothing to indicate the crime occurred in the stable and that they were satisfied Linson was not in west Indianapolis on Saturday.[300]

Ben was reported as having a strong interest in the case, which buoyed the spirits of the neighbors of the Gebhardts.[301] He and Detective Timothy Splan were reported on August 6th to be quietly pursuing a clew.[302]

---

299 *The Indianapolis Journal* – July 28, 1895
300 *The Indianapolis News* – July 29, 1895, p.7
301 *The Indianapolis Journal* – July 30, 1895
302 *The Indianapolis Journal* – August 6, 1895

Although several arrests were made in this case, this case remained unsolved. This high profile murder case went cold for a year until September 25, 1896, when a report came that a convict in Michigan City prison, Alfred Knapp, confessed to the crime. He had been sentenced October 3, 1895 for an attempt rape on Bessie Draper, age 13. While in prison, Knapp confessed to his cell mate, who was serving a year. The cell mate made an affidavit to the prison warden. Sheriff Womack of the west Indianapolis police was advised of this development.

For some reason, no action was taken by the Indianapolis Police Department to follow up on this, as can be determined. The case again reared its head, February 26, 1903 when Knapp again made a confession, this time to Mayor Bosch of Hamilton, Ohio. This time he confessed to the following five murders:

January 21, 1894, killed Emma Littleman in a lumberyard, Cincinnati.

August 1, 1894, killed May Eckert, Cincinnati.

August 7, 1894, killed my wife Jennie Connors Knapp under the canal bridge, Cincinnati.

July 1895, I killed Ida Gebhard.

December 22, 1902, I killed my wife Anna Knapp in Hamilton, Ohio.

Sworn to before me this 26th day of February, 1902: C.F. Bosch, Mayor. [303]

---

[303] *The Indianapolis News* – February 26, 1903, p.1

Alfred Knapp [304]

On August 19, 1904 at 12:09 a.m., Alfred A. Knapp was electrocuted in the Ohio State Prison.[305]

---

[304] http://www.drc.ohio.gov/web/executed/large/executed18.jpg

[305] *The Indianapolis News* – August 19, 1904, p.1

Detectives McGuff and Thornton arrested John W. Fisher the evening of October 15, 1895. He was charged with killing Daniel Fox in Louisville. He said that Fox had threatened his life several times and came to his home to assault him, when Fisher shot Fox in self-defense.[306]

[306] *The Indianapolis News* – October 16, 1895, p.7

DIAMONDS IN HIS LINE

DETECTIVE THORNTON'S EXPERIENCE WITH THESE ROBBERIES.

Unusual Cases That Were All Reported on Sunday—A Woman Who Returned a Stone.

"Diamond robberies is my 'long suit' when they are reported on Sunday," remarked detective Ben Thornton, the colored sleuth hound of the Indianapolis 'fly cop' force. Having thus delivered himself Mr. Thornton elevated a boot to the office table and proceeded with his tale.

[307]

December 15, 1895

The home of James L. Smith, north of the Bright wood neighborhood, was burglarized the morning of October 20th. A gold watch, a violin, a coat and vest and a few dollars in change were stolen. On the floor of the house was found a card, bearing

[307] The Indianapolis Journal – December 15, 1895, p.14 Chronolicamerica.loc.gov

the name of a woman living on Mill Street, with the number of the house. Mr. Smith discovered the robbery a short time after it had happened, and came to police headquarters, bringing the card with him.

The calling card was turned over to detective Ben Thornton, who went to the number mentioned. He showed the card to the woman, whose name it bore, and asked: "To whom did you give this card" “I gave one like it to a man named Carrell a few days ago. He will be here in a few minutes." Thornton took a seat.

It was not long until a man entered, wearing a coat and vest which answered the description of the one stolen from Mr. Smith. Thornton arrested the man. The man’s name was Frank Carrell. He was slated for grand larceny and house breaking.

"I want to know," Carrell asked, 'how you caught on so quick." Thornton produced the card which had been dropped in the house robbed. "Well I'll declare," said Carrell, I thought I was pretty click, but I guess I have a few things to learn. Well, I'm glad that if I had to be arrested a colored man did it."[308]

About 1:15 p.m. on October 23, 1895, two men were seen going into a house owned by Calvin Moorman at 185 Cornell Avenue on the east side of town. A neighbor, brother-in-law of Mr. Moorman saw this and began to investigate. These men had arrived in Indianapolis from Cincinnati the previous day and began committing crimes. They stole some pins and needles to use as a ruse for selling door to door.

If a family wasn't home, they planned on burglarizing the home. One of the men pulled a pistol and fired at the neighbor, missing him. The men started east from there. Harry Rader was riding his bicycle and saw this incident. He gave chase and followed them through various streets until they reached Woodruff Place, then on the far side of Indianapolis.

The suspects boarded a Clifford Avenue street car there and returned to the downtown area. One got off at the Massachusetts Avenue passenger station and

---

[308] *The Indianapolis Journal* – October 20, 1895

the other rode a little farther down the street. The two men met and started west. Mr. Rader had kept the men in sight all this time and at this time he telephoned the police station. In response, a number of patrolmen with Captain Robert Campbell jumped into the patrol wagon and a fast run was made to Michigan Street and Massachusetts Avenue. Upon arrival the police could not find the suspects.

The police deployed from the patrol wagon and finally saw the men again. Michael Ryan, citizen, saw the men and followed them in a buggy. He overtook detectives Ben Thornton and David Richards, who got into the buggy with him. The buggy caught up with the suspects at Meridian and Ohio Streets. The detectives covered the men with their revolvers and the suspects surrendered.

Detective David S. Richards

The suspects gave the names of James C. Requis and Charles Walker. They refused to talk. They were charged with burglary and assault and battery with intent to kill. Superintendent Thomas Colbert praised the officers on their work.[309]

Superintendent Colbert received a letter November 1st from St. Louis police about Charles Walker. His name was

---

[309] *The Indianapolis News* – October 23, 1895, p.7

Charles Miller, a professional burglar who had shot a policeman there, the last time he served a term in prison. They sent his photo from their rogue's gallery to the Indianapolis Police Department.[310] On November 12th, Judge Cox sentenced James Requis and Charles Walker to the penitentiary for two years.[311]

---

[310] *The Indianapolis News* – November 1, 1895, p.4
[311] *The Indianapolis News* – November 13, 1895, p.8

CHAPTER 10: "PUT YOUR HANDS UP OR I WILL SHOOT"

Ben Thornton made this remark to a crowd sitting in the detective's room at the police station in November of 1895. It was one he had made before. "A number of years ago a man who has since reformed and accounted a good citizen had a reputation as a chicken thief that was second to none in the state.

An attempt was made to rob a hen roost in the north part of the city one night, but the robber was frightened away. There had been a good deal of that kind of work going on, and the superintendent was anxious to have it stopped."

Continuing, Ben said, "When I got to the place I found a push-cart that had been left by the thief in his flight. In the cart was a new sole of a shoe. I put the sole in my pocket, just why I don't know, but I thought that it might come in handy sometime and then I started out to find the owner of the push-cart. It was a couple of days before I learned that the push-cart belonged to a well to do firm and I was certain that none of them would be in the chicken business, so the cart must have been stolen. But who stole it? It must be someone familiar with the place, and I continued at my hunt. Then a thought struck me."

"I took the shoe sole to every shoemaker in the city, and asked each if he had made the repairs. At least one mad said it was his work, but he could not remember who he had done the work for. I asked him to try and think of it, and left the sole with him. The next day I called to see him and he remembered the name of the man. Then to find the man I finally located him, and found him hoeing cabbage about two miles in the country. I leaned over the fence and engaged him in conversation. Suddenly I said:

"'Candy, where is the sole of your shoe?'"

"'I pulled it off the other day', he replied, without changing countenance.'

"well, I found it. Let me fit it on for you.'"

"I soon had him covered and marched him back to town. He told me the story. He stole the push-cart and went to the place where he expected to get a lot of fine chickens. He tore the sole off his shoe on the street-car tracks and threw it into the cart, intending to nail it on again as soon as he got home, but when he was frightened away he forgot the shoe sole that resulted in his capture and a term in prison."[312]

The Diamond Thieves

An important case began between 5 and 6 p.m. on New Year's Eve, 1896. A well-dressed young man with a mustache walked into the jewelry store of C.J. Hollis, 81 Massachusetts Avenue and asked to see some diamonds. A woman stood near the door, not paying attention apparently although the purchase was supposed to be for her.

Mr. Hollis placed a tray of diamonds on the show case and the man examined them closely. He told the woman, "I wish you would go over and get your father and see if

[312] *The Indianapolis News* – November 11, 1895, p.5

this will suit him. I expect him to pay half the price."

After 10 minutes had elapsed, the father hadn't arrived and the man made a remark that got Mr. Hollis to look toward the door. When he did, the man grabbed the tray of diamonds and ran out the door, with the store keeper chasing after him yelling "Police!" and "Thief!"

In a short time a crowd had gathered and was chasing the man, who ran around the block three times, with them after him. He threw red pepper into the eyes of some of them, then ran up a stairway. When he emerged, he had changed his hat for a cap.

One pursuer hadn't been thrown off the trail, a citizen named Joseph Haspell. He followed as the man got on a street car and urged the conductor to stop. When he did, Haspell and a Simon Kiser moved in on the suspect. They held him until IPD officers Sergeant Frank Schwab and Patrolmen Woodard, Joshua Spearing, Daniel Haley,

McCarty and Patrick J. Curran[313] arrived and arrested him.

Frank Schwab **Daniel F. Haley**

When taken to police headquarters, the man complained of being kicked to the superintendent, who asked if he wanted to prosecute for assault and battery. The man said, “Oh, no, I guess it’s all right this time”, with a smile. He denied all knowledge of the theft but couldn’t account for the red pepper in his pocket.

At length he admitted taking the diamonds, explaining he couldn’t find work and didn’t want his wife to starve. He gave a name of Dick Wilson from New York City. He said his wife could be located in a

[313] Fired from IPD for conduct unbecoming an officer, January 18, 1897 (Indianapolis News,p.2)

rooming house in West Ohio Street, where she was found. She denied knowing the suspect. Brought to headquarters, she refused to talk and was identified as Annie Adams.

As to the diamonds that were stolen, it contained about $400 worth of stones, some of which had been dropped in the snow. Six were found in Dick Wilson's cap and the crowd found a couple in the snow.

While examining Dick Wilson's possessions, Superintendent Thomas Colbert found on his collar the name "Charles A. Hardin." He recognized it as the express robber. Ben Thornton arrived and Wilson admitted to him that his name was Charles A. Hardin and that he had been arrested for robbing the express company, but was acquitted of the charge. Thornton was

satisfied that Hardin was wanted in Kansas City.[314]

[315]

[314] *The Indianapolis News* – January 1, 1896, p.6

[315] Indianapolis Police Department mugshot.

On January 2nd, a clerk from L.S. Ayres department store identified the couple in jail as the ones who stole a cloak that Annie Adams was wearing when arrested. On January 3rd, Superintendent Colbert received a letter from the Pinkerton Detective Agency of Chicago, with a photograph and record of Charles A. Ketchum, alias Harding. His real name was William "Hob-Nailed" Reilly, well known thief and jewelry sneak, with a long criminal history. His wife, who IPD had in custody was a well-known shoplifter named Minnie Brown. Chicago P.D. had several warrants for his arrest.[316]

---

[316] *The Indianapolis News* – January 3, 1896, p.2

No. ......

Name Annie Adams

Offense G L

Date 12/31/95

Legitimate Occupation ......

Criminal Occupation ......

Nativity U S

Age 36 Height 5-5½ Weight 170

Complexion Light

Eyes Blue Grey

Color of Hair Brown

Color of Beard ......

Scars and Marks Eruption of Skin & pitts in face

Arrested by ......

REMARKS

Caplan & Thornton

[317]

Detective Force as of January 1896

For some time, Indianapolis police had been searching for a gang that had been breaking into empty houses and stealing lead pipes. In one instance, the thieves stole $300 worth of plumbing and sold it for under

---

[317] *The Indianapolis News* – January 18, 1896, p.7

$5.00. They got a lead when Patrolman John P. Boylan arrested a man with a lot of lead pipe, stolen from a house. The man identified Tobias Whitfield as being involved in the theft. Ben Thornton and two policemen went looking for Whitfield on March 5, 1896.

Whitfield spotted the police and ran. Ben pursued him into a house and there, he and Whitfield began fighting. Whitfield was much larger than Ben. Ben was knocked down and Whitfield ran. Thornton was in hot pursuit and the man ran back into the home where another fight ensued. The detective pulled his revolver and threatened to use it. Whitfield said to go ahead and shoot, he wouldn't be taken alive.

At this point, Ben Thornton struck Whitfield with a blow from his "black jack". Whitfield sprang to his feet, grabbed an ax in the yard and advanced on Ben, who tried to use his "billy" club. Whitfield was too strong and escaped.

Police headquarters received word that Whitfield was northwest of Indianapolis in the town of Lebanon, Indiana.

Superintendent Colbert instructed Detective Thornton to go after him and "don't return until you bring the man back with you."

Ben Thornton went home, put on a disguise and left for Lebanon that day. He went to Lebanon police headquarters and picked up two of their officers. They discovered Whitfield walking along the road and drove up to him in a buggy. Whitfield moved over to leg the buggy pass and as he did so, Ben jumped from his seat, landing directly in front of Whitfield, with a cocked pistol close to his face.

"Tobe", Ben said, "I have fooled with you all I am going to. Put your hands up, or I will shoot."

Tobias Whitfield was put off guard by this surprise appearance of Ben Thornton but still put up a fight. The three officers struggled with him but put handcuffs on Whitfield. Ben took him to the train station and seated Whitfield in the agent's office. Soon, an estimated 300 people had arrived, including the mother of Tobias Whitfield. As they were white, the situation was becoming racially charged. Tobias' mother used strong language, threatening the police. As the train pulled into the station, the crowd gathered around Ben and his prisoner. Revolver in hand, Ben put him into a coach.

As the train was nearing Indianapolis, Tobias Whitfield again showed signs of resisting. The detective had had enough at this point. He told Whitfield he had instructions to bring him in and he could take his choice between riding up town in a dead wagon or a patrol wagon. This ended the prisoner's resistance. At 4 p.m. he was locked in his cell.[318]

The J.W. Smith & Son's Bakery at 123 Ft. Wayne Avenue was burglarized on Sunday, April 19, 1896. On April 21st, Ben Thornton arrested Samuel Beard, about 35 for the crime. He had a large number of pennies in his possession.[319] The following morning in Police Court, Beard made his appearance. Ben testified that he had heard that Beard, who lived next door to the bakery, had spent a lot of pennies on Sunday,

---

[318] *The Indianapolis News* – March 8, 1896, p.8
[319] *The Indianapolis News* – April 22, 1896, p.7

but this was not enough evidence for the court, which discharged Beard.[320]

The home of George F. Adams of 148 East New York Street was burglarized of valuable jewelry on April 17, 1896. The jewelry was valued in excess of several thousand dollars.[321] On April 30th, Ben Thornton was in Terre Haute, Indiana, searching for the missing diamonds. He had already searched in Louisville, Jeffersonville, Indiana, Cincinnati, Covington, Kentucky and Lexington, Kentucky looking for them without success.[322]

Detective Ben Thornton, of Indianapolis, was here yesterday in search of the diamonds recently stolen-from the house of G. F. Adams, of Indianapolis. The jewels were valued at $800. Thornton has been In Louisville, Jeffersonville, Cincinnati, Covington and Lexington after them, but has not so far found any trace of them.

The man suspected of the crime, Whit Starr, using the name of Alexander Brockway, made his way to Louisville,

---

320 *The Indianapolis News* – April 23, 1896, p.7
321 *The Indianapolis News* – April 25, 1896, p.7
322 Vigo County Semi-Weekly Express – May 1, 1896

Kentucky, where he was arrested in early May, 1896. The Louisville authorities sent a photo of him to the Indianapolis police so they could recognize him. Before extradition papers could be completed, Starr was released on bond and fled. On May 5th, Starr was again arrested in Louisville. On the afternoon of May 6, 1896, Ben Thornton left town for Louisville, Kentucky. He had been instructed to get Whit Starr and return him to face charges of robbing W.G. Adams.[323]

---

[323] *The Indianapolis News* – May 6, 1896, p.7

No.
Name Whit Storm
Offense Burg & G L
Date May 7/96-
Legitimate Occupation
Criminal Occupation Thief
Nativity US
Age 26 Height 5-8 1/2 Weight 140
Complexion Light
Eyes Light Grey
Color of Hair Sandy
Color of Beard
Scars and Marks
Arrested by Kocher 6/30/96
REMARKS
Thornton 5/7/97-
Mole on left Cheek

[324]

324 Indianapolis Police Department mugshot.

Thornton and Starr returned to Indianapolis, the next day, where Starr, who was termed a “notorious burglar”, went to the grand jury. Thornton, while in Louisville, recovered a gold watch belonging to the victim George F. Adams.[325]

On June 9, 1896, Whit Starr was sentenced to two years in the penitentiary in Criminal Court.[326] On June 27, 1896, Whit Starr escaped from the Marion County Jail by sawing through his cell bars. The jail was supposedly escape proof.[327] He was said in 1903 to be the only man to ever successfully saw his way out of this jail.

---

[325] *The Indianapolis News* – May 8, 1896, p.6
[326] The Indianapolis News – June 9, 1896, p.2
[327] The Indianapolis News – June 27, 1896, p.4

Detective Frank Wilson -1896

John Price, a farmer living three miles outside Terre Haute, Indiana, was robbed by a young man named "Doc" Smith, after giving him a ride. Smith grabbed Price's purse containing over $400 and took off. After making a report with Terre Haute Police Detective McCray, it was learned that Smith was on his way to Indianapolis with two "notorious" women, via train. McCray followed them to Indianapolis.

IPD Detective Frank Wilson, assigned to this case, met with Ben Thornton, May 24, 1896 and as "Doc" Smith was African-

American, he asked if Ben could assist him in finding the suspect. Within three minutes of getting the suspect's description, Thornton had him in custody. He was arrested in a saloon on Indiana Avenue.

Thornton found a total of $426 hidden on Smith. Detective McCray took Smith back to Terre Haute to face trial for highway robbery.[328]

On July 7, 1896, Ben Thornton apprehended Edward Freeman and charged him with burglary. Freeman had on a suit of clothes which was stolen from the home of W.M. Fryberger. An alligator pocketbook, stolen from the home of Mrs. Graham of 79 West Vermont Street, was in his pocket. Other items of suspected stolen property were in his room. Police suspected he had been doing most of the burglaries in the city over the past few months.[329]

On July 25, 1896, Ben made a trip to Greensburg, Indiana and returned with several diamonds worth $1,000. They were

---

[328] *The Indianapolis Journal* – May 24, 1896

[329] *The Indianapolis News* – July 7, 1896, p.7

stolen from Gus Rahke. IPD had received information that the diamonds might be in the possession of John Hittle, a wealthy man. Ben found Hittle in a camping party seven miles from Greensburg. Hittle said that the diamonds had been pawned to him for $180. The stones were at his mother's home in Greensburg, who handed them over.[330]

John Hittle came to Indianapolis on August 3rd and surrendered himself. He was arraigned on a charge of grand larceny and pleaded not guilty.

It was reported in the News that on September 4th, John Thornton of Terre Haute, brother of Ben Thornton, was badly scalded that afternoon at the North rolling-mills. It was caused when Thornton threw cold water on hot cinders, causing an explosion.[331] This is the only evidence of John Thornton that has been found.

On October 6, 1896, The United Order of Odd Fellows heled their 43rd annual meeting at Masonic Hal. Ben Thornton had the honor of introducing the keynote speaker,

---

[330] *The Indianapolis News* – July 25, 1896, p.7
[331] *The Indianapolis News* – September 4, 1896, p.9

Indianapolis Mayor Thomas Taggart. He did so by introducing him as the "genial mayor of the city who would proceed to throw open the gates."[332]

Indianapolis Police received word from Cincinnati on November 25, 1896 that they had arrested Harvey Singleton. Singleton was wanted by IPD for the murder of Calvin Vorhees, on Indiana Avenue, October 12, 1896. The department sent Ben Thornton to Cincinnati to identify him and bring him back.[333] Unfortunately, when Ben arrived at the Cincinnati Police Department, the man they had in custody was not Harvey Singleton, who Ben knew on sight.

On November 28th, the police at Harrodsburg, Kentucky, hometown of Harvey Singleton informed IPD that they had him in custody. Ben departed for Harrodsburg. On December 1st, Ben telegraphed IPD from Harrodsburg, saying he would be leaving at 1 p.m. with Harvey Singleton. [334]

---

332 *The Indianapolis News* – October 6, 1 896, p.8

333 *The Indianapolis News* – November 5,1896, p.8

334 *The Indianapolis News* – December 1, 1896, p.7

Benjamin Thornton - 1896

Departmental Portrait

On December 26, 1896, at 41 Roanoke Street, an assault took place at the home of Lulu Shores. Smith Payne stabbed Arthur Sweenie in the left breast, a serious wound. Lulu and another woman at the home were planning on leaving town with an vaudeville company. Sweenie, was in a back room with Lulu when Smith Payne, who she called her husband, entered. He lunged at Sweenie with his knife, then fled. Smith Payne left Indianapolis.

On December 29th, the Indianapolis Police Department received a telegram from the marshal of Danville, Indiana, saying that Payne was there. Detectives Martin McGuff and Ben Thornton were dispatched to arrest him. When they arrived in Danville they found that Payne had been at the home of Emma Reynolds, but had left there for Peoria, Illinois.

The detectives calculated that they could make as much time by coming back to Indianapolis than by following the fugitive from Danville. They hopped a freight train bound for Indianapolis. A few miles outside of Danville, the train crew discovered them. Although they explained their business, they were put off the train. Ben managed to jump back on the rear of the train and rode into Indianapolis, but McGuff was left by the side of the tracks and walked back into Danville.

The next morning, December 30th, Ben went back to Danville, picked up McGuff and the two went on to Greencastle, Indiana, west of Danville. They had heard Payne had stopped there. They heard he went to the home of an uncle and there, the detectives captured him. By January 1, 1897, Sweenie was making a good recovery.[335] Smith Payne was sentenced to 1-14 years in prison, serving until January 14, 1901 when he was paroled.

In other cities throughout the country colored men act as detectives and policemen. One of the best known colored officers in the United States is Detective Ben Thornton, of Indianapolis. Thornton has been identified with the Police Department of the Hoosier capital for the past quarter of a century, and no man in that city is more dreaded by professional crooks who tour the country. Thornton frequently comes to this city after prisoners who are wanted at Indianapolis. He is known to detectives in all cities of the first class in the country.

The Cincinnati Enquirer, 17 Jan 1897, Sun, Page 16

[335] *The Indianapolis News* – January 1, 1897, p.2

The Murder of Fireman Frank Redmond

One of the biggest murder cases in Indianapolis history up to this time began the night of January 22, 1897. Frank M. Redmond was a pipeman of Hose Company No. 8, stationed at the engine-house at Massachusetts Avenue, near St. Clair Street. He was shot and killed that night and nothing was known of his killer or killers immediately.

The shooting occurred about 6:30 p.m. Two men entered the second hand store of Job Eldridge, 275 Massachusetts Avenue. Both wore slouch hats pulled down on their heads. One wore a handkerchief or muffler, which hid the lower part of his face. They asked Eldridge to let them see a lap robe, which he did. The two men left, saying they were going to drive their buggy around front.

Eldridge didn't like their appearance or actions, thinking they might try and rob him. He was hiding his pocketbook when the men reentered the store and one of them grabbed him. He struck him with the butt of the revolver. Eldridge began resisting and the two of them fell against a partition wall separating his business and that of a restaurant at 277 Massachusetts Avenue, owned by Laura Randolph. She heard the noise of her china rattling and Mr. Eldridge's cries.

Mrs. Randolph and a customer went to the entrance of the Eldridge store and she screamed "Murder! Thieves!", which aroused the neighborhood. One of the men said as they ran, "Did you get the money?" They separated as one of them fell. The one who fell got up and ran toward an alley on the opposite side of Massachusetts Street.

Redmond and two other firemen, Philip Kile and James Cassady, began chasing him toward the alley, which was the first alley east of Park Avenue. Redmond was about 20 feet ahead of the other firemen as he pursued the man into an alley. The Fire Company sent an alarm to police headquarters. Police responded by sending a patrol wagon containing six policemen and detectives Timothy Splan, Frank Wilson, Martin McGuff, David Richards and John Kaehn at full speed.

Detective John Kaehn - 1896

FRANK M. REDMOND.
SCENE OF ATTEMPTED ROBBERY. SCENE OF THE MURDER.

As soon as Kile and Cassady entered the alley, they heard a loud gunshot and saw a flash. Redmond staggered and fell. The man he was chasing ran north in the alley and disappeared. Redmond was carried to the engine-house, 300 feet away. There, Redmond was placed on a cot and died within 10 minutes of being shot. It appeared he had been shot with a .32 bullet between the eyebrows.

The police arrived at this time. They decided to use bloodhounds in tracking the criminals. Superintendent Thomas Colbert telegraphed Powers & Harris, of Noblesville for a pair of hounds and they said they would ship them, with arrival time of 3:30. Police read a description of the men at roll-call and IPD sent their sergeants out in buggies to search the outskirts of Indianapolis.

The bloodhounds reached Indianapolis at 3:30 a.m. A squad of police composed of Sergeants Christian Kruger and Frank Schwab, Patrolmen Wallace and Jesse Streit and Detectives Ben Thornton and Jerry Kinney, accompanied the dogs.

The dogs lost the trail after a short while. The police figured he accosted someone and left on a vehicle. On the following morning, January 23rd, the apparent murder weapon was found by H.C. Page in the first alley south of St. Joseph Street near Ft. Wayne Avenue. It had been fired once.

Two possible clues were found. John G. Kline, who kept a barber shop at 55 Massachusetts Avenue, reported that two men came into his shop at 7:45 p.m. on January 22nd. One stayed outside, the other one came in. His clothes were soiled and the knee of his trousers appeared as if he had been kneeling in the snow. He was tall and wore dark clothes and had a heavy brown mustache. He asked Kline to shave him and cut his mustache off. The barber noticed the man had been shaved already, probably no longer than 10 hours previously.

The man appeared very nervous, while the other man paced up and down outside the shop, as if keeping watch. Kline's descriptions of them matched the ones of Mr. Eldridge, the robbery suspect.[336]

The other clue was a hat, supposed to have been worn by one of the two men, found in Eldridge's store. A Derby style hat, it was brought in St. Louis. It was size 7 1/8, black in color. It came from the store of George Thies, Eight and Pine Streets, St. Louis.[337]

Frank M. Redmond, age 28, was appointed to the Indianapolis Fire Department on August 1, 1894.[338]

By the evening of January 25th, 48 hours had elapsed since the murder and IPD

---

[336] *The Indianapolis News* – January 23, 1897, p.1

[337] Ibid

[338] *The Indianapolis News* – January 23, 1897, p.1

was more skeptical of the Redmond murder being solved. On Saturday night, January 23rd, Ben Thornton boarded a train for St. Louis, taking with him the revolver and a hat, which are supposed to belong to the murderer. The suspect had been shaved at Kline's Barber Shop it was thought and Ben also had his mustache, which was retrieved by Superintendent Thomas Colbert. In the age of DNA, this would have been a valuable clue.

In St. Louis, Ben Thornton called on a hatter, George Thies, at Eighth and Pike Streets, to see if he could identify the person he sold it to. He could not. Thies said the hat had been recently purchased from him, although it was well worn.

Ben went to the St. Louis Police Department to inquire if the revolver had been purchased from any of their pawn shops, second hand stores or firearms stores in the city. St. Louis assigned four detectives to assist Detective Thornton with this. They could think of no man in their city who answered the description of the wanted man. Ben got no results from his efforts and left the hat with the St. Louis police, who would attempt to locate its owner.[339]

A break in the case came when IPD checked on all vehicles that were rented the night of the murder. All names and descriptions of these persons were sent to headquarters. It was determined that an Edward Phillips had rented a horse and buggy from the stable of David R. Marshall, 38 Oak Street, about 8 p.m. Friday night. It had not been returned that night. Patrolmen Kurtz and Milam took a report that the buggy rented from Marshall was in Booth's stable, West Market Street, at 3 a.m., the next morning.

[339] *The Indianapolis News* – January 25, 1897, p.1

Phillips was said to be keeping company with a woman named Laura Alice Spoon, at Illinois and Market Streets. The man described by the stable employees as being with Edward Phillips the night he rented the buggy was identified as Carl Harvey.

Detective Martin McGuff knew Harvey by reputation, having a prison record. Soon, both Phillips and Harvey were under arrest, in separate cells.[340]

[340] *The Indianapolis News* – January 27, 1897, p.2

On June 21, 1897, it was announced that a Tennessee convict named James Burton had confessed to the murder of Frank M. Redmond. He was serving a sentence of three years for a burglary in Nashville. He admitted to Superintendent Colbert that he fired the fatal shot. He was the man in the alley, while Harvey and Phillips committed the actual robbery. His confession was as follows, as related by Colbert:

"He told me that he had arranged with Harvey, whom he knew well in Columbus, to rob old man Eldridge. Harvey had an idea that the old man had a lot of money. He said when they failed and started to run, he found Redmond too close to him. He turned and fired his revolver, which had been given to him by Harvey before the robbery was attempted. He ran through an alley to St. Clair Street and turning east, met Harvey and Phillips. They told him to meet them in front of the Park Theater. Burton then got shaved. Phillips went to the livery stable, got the buggy and met Burton at the Park Theater and drove him to Greenwood, Indiana."[341]

---

[341] *The Indianapolis News* – June 21, 1897, p.4

On June 22, 1897, the grand jury returned two indictments against James Burton, the murderer of Frank Redmond, the other for complicity in the assault and attempted robbery of Job Eldridge.[342]

James Burton was tried in Greenfield, Indiana and found guilty, November 27, 1897. He received a sentence of life imprisonment.[343]

---

[342] *The Indianapolis News* – June 22, 1897, p.2
[343] *The Indianapolis News* – November 29, 1897, p.7

CHAPTER 11:
"REMEMBER OUR ENEMIES!"

Indianapolis Police had been searching for four men who were considered to be a dangerous gang. The men were Albert J. Rabb, 24, William Gleason, 25, Robert Landis, 22 and James Donnelly, 21. They had their headquarters in the room of Rose Shane, 21 Ryan Block.

On January 31, 1897, these men had broken into Newsom's store at Carthage, in Rush County, Indiana. They stole $165 in goods and cash. They were pursued from Knightstown, Indiana by a constable and a man named Scovil.

When they reached the town limits of Irvington (in 2015 this is a neighborhood on the east side of Indianapolis but was a separate town in 1897), a protracted gun battle began. The pursuers had one revolver between them. The gang they were chasing had several weapons.

Volley after volley were fired between these six men, while the citizens of Irvington ran for cover. Both sides finally ran out of ammunition. The suspects entered a street car, which stopped when the conductor realized they were being pursued. They ran northwest from that location and were seen at Ohio Street and the Belt railroad. There, they commandeered a sleigh from Mr. F.W. Yeager and were last seen driving west.

The Indianapolis Police Department was notified and a wagon full of police arrived, but it was too late.[344] James Donnelly was apprehended here, the first member of the gang to be taken into custody.

On February 5, 1897, Detectives Thornton and Jerry Kinney discovered the meeting place of the gang in the Ryan Block. When they went to the room, Rose Shane was washing clothes. As soon as she saw the detectives she recognized Thornton and grabbed a waistcoat hanging on the wall. She stuffed it into the cooking stove. Ben retrieved it and the woman was arrested for receiving stolen property.

---

[344] *The Indianapolis News* – February 1, 1897, p.2

Ben and Detective Kinney then waited in the room for the return of the other members of the gang, from that afternoon until late at night. A man came to the room at 10 p.m. He was followed by the detectives, who first got another man to watch the room and notify the police when the men came in.

At about 1 a.m., police received a message that the men had returned to their room. Bicycle Patrolmen Charles Ware and Jesse Streit were sent to arrest them. They met Sergeant Christian Kruger on their way, who accompanied them. The police arrived at the room and found the lights turned low and the doors barricaded.

Christian Kruger Jesse Streit

Charles Ware

Sergeant Kruger went to the back door, which was barricaded with a chair. Kruger asked for a lamp, which he received from a woman. Streit held it while Kruger, a strong man, kicked the door apart. He took the lamp in his left hand and a revolver in his right into the room.

He saw in the darkness three men crouching behind a bed. One of them raised his head. Sergeant Kruger covered him with his revolver and ordered him to throw down the revolver he had in his own hand. The man, later identified as Gleason, complied.

By now, Patrolmen Ware and Streit were in the room at the foot of the bed. They covered the other men with their weapons. The suspects also were pointing their revolvers at the police. "Drop those guns!", Kruger commanded, leveling his gun at the men. For a moment, nobody moved and then finally, the burglars lost their nerve and threw down their guns.

"Where are the rest of the cops?" asked Landis. "There were only three of us", answered Streit. "Well, if we had known that, there would have been three dead cops now. We thought there were a dozen by the shuffling in the hall."[345]

Christian Kruger, Charles Ware and Jesse Streit received a commendation from the Board of Public Safety on February 15, 1897, the first in the history of the police department.

The three men arrested were suspects who shot when discovered in a grocery in Walcott Street and are the same ones who shot at the constables during the fight in Irvington the previous Sunday. A large quantity of burglars tools were found in Rose Shane's room, along with blasting powder and fuses. Goods stolen from a store in Carthage, Indiana the previous Saturday were also found.[346]

These four men were arraigned February 10th on for robbery at Carthage and sent to jail at Connersville, Indiana. They were wanted in six other cities according to IPD.[347] On March 16, 1897, at Rushville, Indiana, Walter Donnelly pleaded guilty and was sentenced to three years in prison at

345 *The Indianapolis News*, April 9, 1898, p.2
346 *The Indianapolis News* – February 6, 1897
347 *The Indianapolis News* – February 10, 1897, p.6

Jeffersonville. Albert J. Rabb, William Gleason and Robert Landis were sentenced March 12th, and were also here, accompanied by Detectives Kinney and Thornton.[348]

On March 6, 1897, Essie Thornton gave a dinner party at noon for Representative Gabriel L. Jones at her home, 295 Bright Street. Present were General Jasper Packard, Senator Elias M. Rinear, Representatives Elliott of Marion County, Ross, Butler, Morgan, Blankenship, Linck, Hedgecock and Eichhorn, Councilman John A. Puryear, Dr. Pettijohn and Charles H. Lanier.

Puryear served in the House from 1892-1897. Gabriel L. Jones, a schoolteacher who advocated equal educational opportunities for African-American children, was elected in 1896 to the Indiana House.[349]

---

348 *The Indianapolis News* – March 16, 1897, p.2

349 *The Indianapolis Journal* – March 7, 1897,

Benjamin Thornton's Arson Investigation

At 3 a.m. on April 29, 1897, the stable of J.C. Adams, rear of 750 North Delaware Street, was almost destroyed by fire. Merchant Policeman Sam McClure saw a man standing on a barn adjoining the stable just before the fire broke out. He had a lighted match in his hand and had broken a window. McClure saw him throw the match in the window to light the hay on fire.

Sam McClure fired twice at the man on the shed. The bullets went wide and the man jumped off the barn and over a fence. The fire broke out moments later. James Jones, employee of Mr. Adams, was sleeping in the shed at the time, heard the window break and was burned on his face and hands while getting the horses out. The property loss was $500.[350]

Henry S. Fraser, of 754 North Delaware Street, was awoken by the gunshots and was one of the first people on the scene. Fraser ran to his own stable to find his employee, a William Edwards. He

---

[350] *The Indianapolis News* – April 29, 1897, p.8

could not find Edwards. He claimed he was busy setting the horses in the burning stable free when he appeared on the scene.

While investigating the case, William Edwards, a coachman in the employ of Fraser told Ben Thornton that he was in the loft in the company of a woman when the fire broke out. Ben went to see the woman, who denied she was near Mr. Fraser's stable on the night of the fire.

Ben Thornton examined the burned barn and noticed two fragments of partially burned matches on the window sill where the arsonist had been seen. The previous fall, he had investigated the arson of a Mr. McKee's barn and found matches at the scene. He did a study and found that these types of matches were made in Sweden.

They were of a yellowish color and contained more than an ordinary parlor match. The McKee barn was located just across from Fraser's barn. Now, he found the same kind of matches in the burned out remains of J.C. Adams' barn. He also found the same types of matches in the pockets of William Edwards.[351]

A box of "Swedish matches" as they are still called. They were the first safety matches in the world, manufactured by the Lundstrom Brothers.

Ben arrested Edwards the night of the fire and charged him with arson. Edwards had been employed by Fraser for two years. The police said that he had been an arson suspect for some time and that there had been fires in the neighborhoods he had previously been employed at. They also

[351] *The Indianapolis News* – May 29, 1897 & The Cincinnati Enquirer, May 30, 1897

believed the fires of the barns of Winfield Miller, Fred Mayer, Cortland Van Camp, Henry Drew and L.S. Ayres were arson cases.[352]

Edwards said "The charge against me is false. I never burned a barn in my life." He was scheduled to appear in Police Court on May 7, 1897.[353] Mr. Fraser testified during the five day trial that he had made a special order for the matches from his grocer. On May 28th, Ben Thornton testified at length about his study of certain matches which figure in this case.

---

352 *The Indianapolis News* – April 30, 1897, p.7

353 *The Indianapolis News* - May 7, 1897, p.2

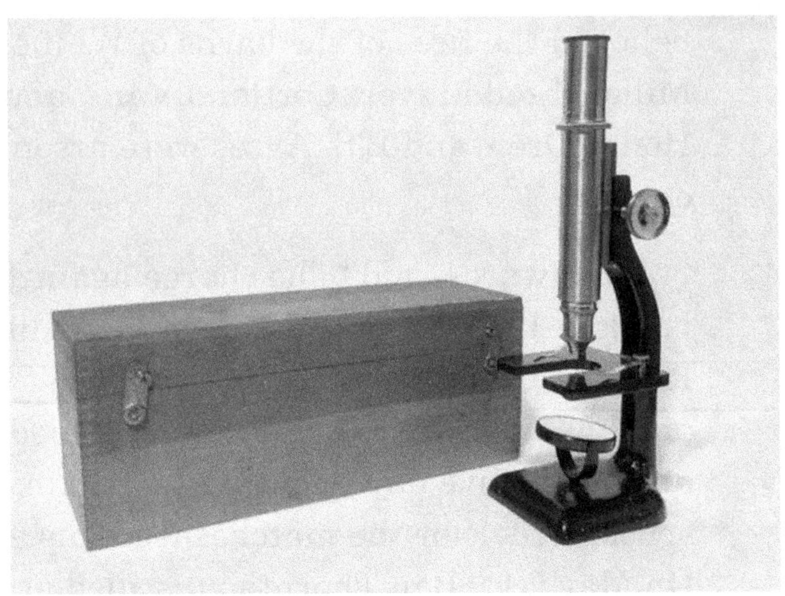

An 1890's microscope similar to what Detective Thornton would have used in the arson case.

He said that since last fall, he has been making a special study of matches, under the microscope and otherwise, trying to find clues in arson cases.[354] At the end of the trial, William Edwards was exonerated in Criminal Court. The evidence was judged to be largely circumstantial. [355] This case is noteworthy for Detective Ben Thornton's use of forensic science in a criminal trial.

---

[354] *The Indianapolis News* – May 29, 1897, p.3
[355] *The Indianapolis News* – June 3, 1897, p.2

On October 27, 1897, the Board of Safety appointed Thomas F. Colbert, previously the Superintendent of Police, as Chief of Detectives. The detectives that would work for him were Jeremiah Kinney, Benjamin Thornton, Timothy Splan, Thomas L. Stout and Frank Wilson.[356]

The morning of October 29, 1897 for Ben Thornton started off with him bicycling to headquarters after having his breakfast. He stopped off on Indiana Avenue to get something for his noon lunch. While waiting for it to be prepared he went to the home of a William Owen, 155 Indiana Avenue. He was wanted for stealing $45 worth of property. The man was home and said he would go to the police station.

Mr. Owen's sister told him, "You had better wash your face before you go." Owen went into a rear room and Ben saw him jump from the second story window and start running. Ben ran for his bicycle and gave chase. For a while, both men began running up and down alleys. Then Owen started jumping fences and running through yards. Ben couldn't get his bike over the fences, so

---

[356] *The Indianapolis News* – October 28, 1897, p.2

he leaned it against a home and started a foot pursuit.

Ben considered himself a fast sprinter, but he couldn't keep up with William Owen. Ben fired his revolver to draw a crowd. About 50 school children heard the pistol and joined in the chase. If Ben lost sight of his quarry, the children would find him and say, "There he goes, Ben, around this way." For 40 minutes Ben Thornton chased Mr. Owen through the neighborhood, before finally overtaking him and putting him in jail.[357]

Ben Goes to Kansas City

Ben packed his things and left the evening of November 29, 1897 for Kansas City, Missouri. He was sent to bring back Thomas Coddlington, alias "Texas Tom", wanted in Indianapolis for stealing bicycles. The complaint had been made October 26th by Frank Staley of the Indiana Bicycle Company. The Kansas City police department wrote IPD that they had arrested Thomas Coddlington, alias "Texas Tom", who was a rifle shooter and pistol juggler.

---

[357] *The Indianapolis News* – October 28, 1897, p.7

Name Thos Caddington
Alias.
Offense G L
Date Dec 22 "97
Legitimate Occupation Cook
Criminal Occupation
Nativity U S
Age 34 Height 5-7½ Weight 150
Complexion Dark
Eyes Grey
Color of Hair D Brown
Color of Beard Mustache Brown
Scars and Marks
Square and Compass
Arrested by Kinney Thornton

REMARKS:

Square and Compass on left arm and Star. Bald Spot on back crown of head

[358]

---

358 Indianapolis Police Department mugshot.

The Kansas City police were doubtful of gaining a conviction. Indianapolis Police thought they could get a conviction.[359] On December 1, 1897, before Judge Spitz in Kansas City, "Texas Tom" was arraigned on the charge of bringing stolen good into the state. The judge informed him that the case was dismissed and he was a free man.

Coddlington gave a slight smile and was starting to leave when he was halted by Ben Thornton's hand. He informed him he had extradition papers from Governor Stephens for his arrest as a fugitive from justice.

"Texas Tom" had a hard time apparently dealing with being arrested by Ben and implored a local officer to go with him as far as the train station. By 1:15 p.m. he was on his to Indianapolis.[360]

Ben brought Coddlington back to Indianapolis on December 2nd. He also brought back five stolen bicycles.[361] Coddlington did plead guilty to petit larceny

---

[359] *The Indianapolis News* – November 30, 1897, p.7

[360] The Kansas City Journal – December 2, 1897, p.10

[361] *The Indianapolis News* – December 3, 1897, p.5

in one case on January 22, 1898. He was sentenced to one year in the work-house.[362]

The Police Department's Identification Bureau

In 1898, the Indianapolis Police Department set up its first Criminal Identification Bureau. It used a criminal identification system known as the Bertillon system. This system, named for the French police photographer who developed it, would be widely used across the United States to identify criminals.

It consisted of taking a number of measurements of the head and various other body parts, the width and length of hands, feet, etc. which were supposed to be a method of making positive identification. Jerry Kinney and Benjamin Thornton set this system up for IPD and it was used until 1931 when it was finally replaced by the forensic science of fingerprints.[363]

A box of instruments for use with the Bertillon system arrived at police

---

[362] *The Indianapolis News* – January 22, 1898, p.11

[363] "Indianapolis Police Department – A Proud Tradition of Service", (2000), p.19

headquarters in March 1898. IPD set aside two rooms in their headquarters to house the Criminal Identification Bureau.[364]

Other aspects of the Criminal Identification Bureau included photographing arrested subjects. Hundreds of these "mugshots" from the 1890's still survive in the police department archives.

Ben left Indianapolis the morning of January 29th for Cairo, Illinois. He was going to pick up James Wilder, arrested there for the murder of Otto Minger in September of 1897. Going with Ben was C. Fred Kissel.[365] After arriving in Cairo, they found that the man in custody was not James Wilder, but Will Bradley. Bradley was wanted in Indianapolis for stealing a bicycle, but was held in Cairo for a more serious charge.

---

[364] The Indianapolis News – March 24, 1898, p.9

[365] *The Indianapolis News* – January 29, 1898, p.1

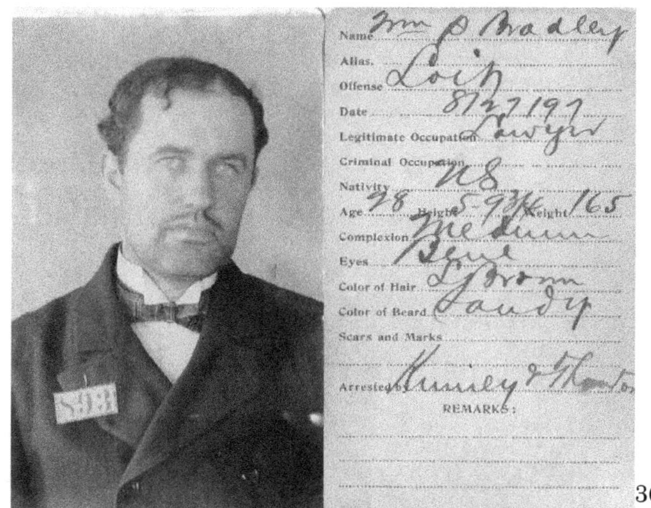

[366]

William P. Bradley

C. Fred Kissel returned with a story that said Ben was ignored by the Cairo Chief of Police, only speaking to Kissel, who went on the trip as the employer of Minger, the murder victim. Kissel also reported that due to the color of his skin,

Ben was prevented from coming back with him the night of January 29th and was told to wait until January 31st, when a train reserved for African-Americans would leave. Further, Ben couldn't find lodging, finally being taken in by an African-American family. Lastly, Kissel was refused

[366] Indianapolis Police Department mug

permission twice to buy whiskey for Ben Thornton.[367]

When he returned, in response to the story of his alleged discrimination, Ben said that Kissel was probably joking. "I was never better treated in my life", Ben said. "The chief offered to take me about the city Sunday. I stayed at the best hotel in the town. Once or twice we had difficulty purchasing drinks, but otherwise, everything was fair."[368]

The John H. Brown Case

There was a rash of break-ins of grocery stores and private residences on the south and southeast part of Indianapolis. The town of Irvington, on Indianapolis' far eastside, also had about 30 places broken into, silverware and numerous other items being stolen.

Ben Thornton was put on the case. After a week of effort, he, along with Detectives Adolph Asch and Thomas F. Dugan, made the arrest of one John Brown,

---

[367] *The Indianapolis News* – January 31, 19898, p.3

[368] *The Indianapolis News* – February 1, 1898,

alias Chauncey K. Fuller. He wasn't able to find much on Brown's accomplices however.

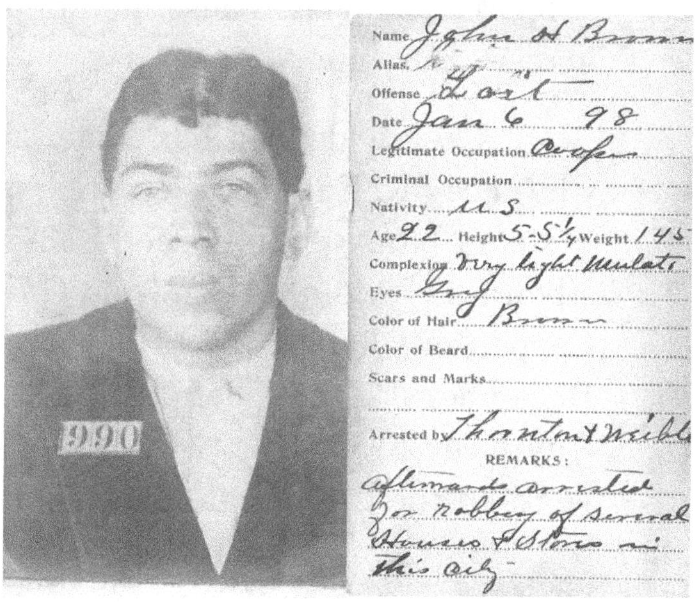
Name John H Brown
Alias
Offense
Date Jan 6 98
Legitimate Occupation
Criminal Occupation
Nativity U S
Age 22 Height 5-5¼ Weight 145
Complexion Very light Mulatto
Eyes Grey
Color of Hair Brown
Color of Beard
Scars and Marks
Arrested by Thornton & Weible
REMARKS:
afterwards arrested for robbery of several Houses & Stores in this city

[369]

On February 2nd, Brown was offered a deal where if he gave up information on his accomplices and help recover the stolen goods, he would receive no more than three years in prison, pleading guilty to petit larceny rather than grand larceny. He directed them to a certain house on Draper Street. Three wagon loads of stolen articles were recovered there. Brown also said that the gang had rented a safety deposit box in a bank, which reportedly amazed Ben

369 Indianapolis Police Department mugshot.

Thornton. Brown said the names of the other gang members were John Burris and John Wehrmeyer. These men fled after the arrest of Brown.

A safety deposit box under the name of Chauncey K. Fuller was located at the Fletcher bank. It contained $167 worth of silver and jewelry stolen from C.F. Carpenter's house, 1529 Hoyt Avenue, December 25, 1897. John Brown, alias Chauncey K. Fuller was sentenced to three years in the Indiana Reformatory, February 3, 1898.[370]

Ben Thornton visited the home of John Wehrmeyer, 1706 Draper Street and arrested Mrs. Elsie Wehrmeyer on February 5th. She could not make a reasonable explanation for the property in her home and refused to say where her husband was.

[370] *The Indianapolis News* – February 3, 1898, p.7

Thomas F. Dugan

On February 6th, armed with a warrant, Detectives Asch and Dugan raided the home 1706 Draper Street address. They recovered several hundred dollars of stolen property, enough to fill two wagons. Much of the loot was stolen from homes in Irvington during the winter. A large quantity of cigars, groceries and clothing, stolen in the southeast part of Indianapolis was also recovered. Mrs. Wehrmeyer pleaded not guilty on February 7th.[371] She was released by the grand jury, due to insufficient evidence, March 21st.[372]

---

371 *The Indianapolis News* – February 7, 1898, p.7
372 *The Indianapolis News* – March 21, 1898, p.10

Police learned the men went to Decatur, Illinois. To lure them in, letters were sent through the mail, addressed to the men. They went to the post office for their mail, where the police of Decatur arrested them.[373]

New Police Headquarters Building

For a number of years, the current headquarters of the Indianapolis Police Department had been overcrowded. In September of 1897, police were moved to a vacant building on the other side of Pearl and Alabama Streets, across from their

---

[373] *The Indianapolis News* - March 24, 1898, p.2

current location. Prisoners were taken across the street from the police lockup to the Marion County Jail.

The building was finished the week of March 3, 1898. It was three stories tall and was built on the same footprint as the previous one. It would stand until the fall of 1962 when it was torn down.[374]

The Struggle to Serve Their Country

For many years, there had been African-American companies in the Indiana State National Guard. One of which, known as the Thornton Guards, was Company M in the 3rd Regiment of the Indiana National Guard. Composed of 58 Indianapolis men, it was organized as the Ross Guards, in April 1886. It was reorganized as the Thornton Guards, in the spring of 1890.[375]

These companies were kept separate from the white members of the Indiana National Guard. On January 15, 1896, Governor James A. Mount detached the two African-American companies from the Indiana National Guard. They continued to

---

[374] The Indianapolis News – March 3, 1898

[375] *The Indianapolis News* – July 26, 1 895, p.2

drill on their own. This was a very sore spot with the African-American members of the Indianapolis community.

On April 8, 1898, 200 of the estimated 3,000 African-Americans of voting age met in the Odd Fellow's Hall on Indiana Avenue to try and take action about this policy of segregation. War with Spain would start in 17 days and the men in the hall did not want to be kept out of it.

At some point during the meeting, Ben Thornton stated that he understood what was going on and why it was done. He said the African-American men were themselves to blame, that they should have done something with the former administration of Governor Claude Matthews (1893-1897). He blamed the present administration as well. He called Governor James A. Mount a "2 cent governor." He received applause when he declared that he believed in voting for men regardless of party.

The best speech given that evening was by the Elder J.W. Carr, pastor of the Second Baptist Church. "Now what is to be done?", he exclaimed.

"Remember our enemies!", shouted Ben Thornton.

"That's right, Brother Thornton," exclaimed Mr. Carr. "Remember them so well that they will not forget us." Resolutions were passed by the leaders of the meeting.[376]

The proposition made this night was not accepted by the Governor or Adjutant-General Core. Instead, they were formed into a separate African-American battalion, to include the two Indianapolis companies and one that was being formed at Marion, Indiana.

For several days, Detectives Jerry Kinney, Timothy Splan and Ben Thornton had been watching a man named Thomas Ford. They thought he was behind burglaries on the north side of town. They obtained a warrant and on May 7, 1898, searched his home in the early morning. They found three gold watches on a roof beam in his shed. Ben found three silver watches among papers under a stove, covered with coal, on the floor of the shed. These

[376] *The Indianapolis News* – April 9, 1898, p.16

were identified by five north side residents who had been burglarized.[377] [378]

The trial of Thomas Ford began May 24th and was enlivened by a sharp exchange involving Ben Thornton. Attorney Newton Harding began a sharp cross-examination of Thornton. Ben got the impression that the attorney was intimating that he had entered the serial number of a watch into his memorandum book *after* he had found it. This set off Ben's short temper and he said some things in response.

Judge McCray interrupted but Ben would not be stopped. The judge pounded his gavel and said "I must protect this court." Ben shouted "It's your duty to protect the witness, too!" The judge said "Mr. Thornton, I'll have to fine you. Mr. Clerk, enter a fine-."

However, the clerk wasn't present. He was sent for and when he returned to court, the judge only said, "Gentlemen, proceed with your evidence."[379] On June 1, 1898, Thomas Ford was found guilty of grand

---

377 *The Indianapolis News* – May 7, 1898, p.11
378 *The Indianapolis News* – June 1, 1898, 9
379 *The Indianapolis News* – May 24, 1898, p.8

larceny in Criminal Court and sentenced to 1-14 years in the Indiana Reformatory.

Inmate Revolt at the Jail

A dangerous situation at the Marion County Jail, located directly across from Indianapolis Police Department headquarters, began during Sunday services, May 29th about 11 a.m. Turnkey Chapman had went upstairs to let out several women from the W.C.T.U (Women's Christian Temperance Union), who had been holding religious services on the second floor. While they went down to the first floor, Chapman took a look around the west corridor to see if everything was all right.

He felt someone slipping up behind him and soon the barrel of a revolver was pointed in his face by Harry Church, a prisoner. Chapman had keys to all the doors and in an instant, stepped to an open window and threw them outside. Church cursed and threatened to "put his lights out."

At that time, Harry Warner, another prisoner, stepped in from the north corridor with a drawn revolver, accompanied by Carl Krauel. Krauel had been sawing away at a bar in one of the windows on the north side of the jail.

MARION COUNTY JAIL.

380

All three prisoners, Church, Warner and Krauel, were among the worst prisoners in the jail, all being arrested for post office robbery.

Krauel had cut through one bar and another one between the south corridor and west corridor had been sawed off during the morning. It was believed this is how these men reached the point where they took Turnkey Chapman prisoner.

---

380 "Hyman's Handbook of 1907"

While Church held Chapman, Warner brought the other prisoners into line and marched them into the north corridor. A trustee, viewing from the bars into the north cell-house saw that something was wrong and gave the alarm. So did William Jasper, aid to Sheriff Thomas P. Shufelton.

Harry Warner heard the shouts of warning, rushed to the bars and ordered Turnkey Chapman to tell the trustees to come upstairs. He repeated this order, this time bringing the other prisoners in line to the bars, while holding a gun on them.

James Klinger, another trustee, jumped over the rail of the walk on the second floor of the jail floor, falling 15 feet to the floor below. He ran for the prisoner's bathroom, keeping out of the line of fire, and accompanied by William Jasper, cried for help. The son of Sheriff Shufelton heard them and ran for his father, who was in a barber shop on Virginia Avenue.

Warner shouted to the men in the bathroom below that he had all the keys to the jail and he would kill them if they didn't come upstairs. They fell for his trick and came up. Klinger was ordered to get on his knees and pray, which he did. Harry Church meanwhile, was marching the turnkey up and down the corridor, threatening to kill him repeatedly.

When Sheriff Shufelton got word of the situation at the jail, he ran to the jail, while his young son notified police headquarters. Superintendent James Quigley and the men in his office came over to help. The sheriff got a Winchester and climbed a ladder to the second floor. Police found the keys in the grass and got into the building.

Sheriff Shufelton fired a shot to frighten the hostage takers and realizing they had failed, the three prisoners they let Chapman throw his one remaining key, to the inside door of the first floor, out the window. Chapman advised them to give up their weapons. Church asked if they would be punished if they surrendered and Chapman promised they would not be hurt, giving his sworn oath that the sheriff would not hurt them.

Sheriff Shufelton unlocked the downstairs door and let out the terrified women of the W.C.T.U. Then he, accompanied by Deputy Sheriff Jasper, Superintendent Quigley, Sergeant Corrigan, Detective Benjamin Thornton and one or two others, rushed upstairs.

Chapman had the three prisoners lined up against the wall with their hands held high. As reported by *The Indianapolis News*, when the door to this corridor was opened, the Sheriff, closely followed by Ben Thornton, rushed in and attacked the hostage takers.

Church was hit over the head with the Sheriff's Winchester rifle, while Ben clubbed them over the head with his club. The rest of the officers joined in at this point. The prisoners were battered to the floor where the beating continued. They yelled for mercy but the beating didn't stop until the men grew tired.

Jailer Chapman, who broke his promise, had bruised knuckles from his part of the beating and Sheriff Shufelton's hand was bruised.

After the authorities regained control, the sheriff attempted to determine how the guns were placed in the prisoner's possession. Several theories were put forward. During the beating, one of the prisoners said a "Tom Carter" had given them the weapons, but would not talk further after being placed in their cells.

Other prisoners thought the guns were probably given to the men the previous Friday while the corridors were being scrubbed. Another story said that a young woman had promised to marry one of the three men when he got out and that she managed to smuggle the revolvers in last week.[381]

On June 2nd, it took a Federal jury only 10 minutes to find the Church gang, namely Harry Church, James Downing, Charles Howard and Harry Warner, who robbed the Lebanon post office, guilty. They were going to the Ohio penitentiary, where they would draw the limit, five years at hard labor.

There was some sympathy given in the public for the beating of the prisoners. Ben Thornton stated on June 2nd that the accusations of cruelty were exaggerated and false as far as they apply to him. He had no

---

[381] *The Indianapolis News* – May 30, 1898, p.6

sympathy for the hostage takers, who would have killed their prisoners if they were successful. Ben claimed the prisoners had been laughing because they escaped greater punishment for their attempted escape.[382]

Arrest of a Murder Suspect

On May 31st, on Clinton Street, Chief of Detectives Thomas Colbert and Ben Thornton arrested John C. Johnson, 27, who was wanted in Grape Creek, Illinois for the murder of Ballard Johnson. It occurred at a miners dance on May 25th. Johnson admitted to the detectives he killed him, but it was in self-defense.[383]

Stake Out at the Denison Hotel

On the morning of August 26, 1898, Detective Ben Thornton and acting Detective Smith were on what now would be called a "stake out", at the Denison Hotel. They started watching at 3 a.m. for a man they suspected of committing numerous thefts from Indianapolis Hotels in the past week, during a Knights of Pythias convention including:

---

382 *The Indianapolis News* – June 2, 1898, p.9

383 *The Indianapolis News* – May 31, 1898, p.9

E.L. Crouch, Fortville, Indiana at Weinberger's Hotel, 1 gold watch.
J.P. Workman, Spencer, Indiana, at Oneida Hotel, gold watch and cash.
W.H. Geyer, Wheeling, W.Va., at English Hotel, watch and money.
J.A. Reed, Kansas City, Mo., at English Hotel, found thief in room but released him.
W.P. Epperson, Colorado City, Co., at English hotel, $4.
DeWitt C. Bolton, Paterson, N.J. at Denison Hotel, $20 & watch.

The thief that J.A. Reed caught in

his room pretended he was a drunk and had entered by mistake. On the morning of August 26th, a man was heard at a female guest's door. She opened the door to find a man on his knees, acting drunk and saying he needed to leave. a chambermaid saw this and a porter grabbed him. They sent for Thornton. The suspect gave his name as Phillip Toney, 56, a brick-layer from Philadelphia, Pennsylvania. He was seemingly drunk, which police saw through as an act. Toney answered the description of the man at Weinberger's Hotel.[384]

---

[384] *The Indianapolis News* – August 26, 1898, p.10

Detectives Ben Thornton and John Weible arrested Charles Alexander on September 23, 1898 on a charge of burglary. They suspected him of breaking into the home of E.M. Campbell in Woodruff Place. [385]

He gave an incorrect home address to throw them off. However, in a moment of serendipity, Ben and his partner Detective Weible were walking down a south side street when they met Alexander's wife and little daughter. The girl spoke to the detectives and said they had arrested her papa. Ben asked her where she lived and the little girl gave their house number.

After placing Alexander in jail, the detectives started to talk over this case and one of them suggested that Alexander might be the burglar who had been entering houses on the south side of town. They also felt that Charles Alexander may have been responsible for the mysterious murder on September 15th, of Christian Wilharm, shot at his home at 1450 Spruce Street.

---

[385] *The Indianapolis News* – September 24, 1898, p.2

CHARLES ALEXANDER. [386]

On September 25th, Detectives Adolph Asch, Thomas F. Dugan, Weible and Ben Thornton went to search Alexander's home at 1712 Linden Street. They brought along Mrs. Mary Moffett, sister of Christian Wilharm. The search revealed two flat-irons and a coffee can, recognized by Mary Moffett as being stolen from the Wilharm house. They also found rubber shoes, popular with burglars and two revolvers in a black coat.

[386] *The Indianapolis News* – September 26, 1898, p.8

The detectives closely questioned the wife of Charles Alexander. On the night of the murder of Wilharm, he did not go to bed, as far as she wife knew. She found him sitting in the kitchen early the next morning. Later that day she was going across the street to borrow some irons and her husband said that there were irons in the closet.

The Wilharm house had been burglarized two weeks prior to the murder and it was theorized the flat irons were stolen at that time. Several witnesses came to police headquarters and said they saw a man resembling Alexander in the Spruce Street neighborhood where Christian Wilharm was murdered. Wilharm's younger brother also said he saw a man that looked like Alexander peering into their home the morning after the murder.

Alexander refused to say anything after his arrest. On the afternoon of September 26th however, he spoke out, strongly stating that he was innocent of the Wilharm murder. He said on the night of the murder he remained in his house all night. He was willing to confess to several burglaries but "I am innocent of the murder of the Wilharm boy."

He stated he was never in the Wilharm house, but robbed the Woodruff Place home and a number of other places on the south side, to the point where he couldn't keep count of them. He said the flat irons and coffee can in question were his property, having had them a long time prior to the murder.[387]

Charles Alexander was found guilty of burglary and petit larceny on December 6, 1898 in Criminal Court.[388] He was sentenced to 2-14 years.[389] Alexander was never charged with the murder of Christian Wilharm and that murder remained unsolved.

Detectives Jerry Kinney and Ben Thornton arrested Paul Rogers on October 21st. He was alleged to have fired three shots at Harry McMullen in the old Hanna house on North Alabama Street, July 22nd. He then

---

387 Ibid.

388 *The Indianapolis News* – December 7, 1898, p.6

389 *The Indianapolis News* – December 10, 1898, p.10

fled and hadn't been seen since the detectives spotted him.[390]

The Indianapolis Police Department decided to investigate an allegation that Detective Thornton assaulted a prisoner named Howard Jones. This prisoner had previously accused Ben Thornton of giving false testimony, whereupon Ben struck him in the face. Superintendent James Quigley said after making an inquiry, he will refer the incident to the Board of Public Safety.[391]

The Board of Public Safety met the morning of November 29th. When interviewed, Ben Thornton said that the man called him a vile name and unjustly accused him. In the heat of passion, he struck him. He pleaded that all policemen were human beings and that sometimes they might forget the rigid requirements of police discipline.

The Board informed Thornton that such conduct was discreditable and if there was a repetition by him or any other officer, they would receive extreme punishment.[392]

---

[390] *The Indianapolis News* – October 22, 1898, p.11
[391] *The Indianapolis News* – November 28, 1898, p.9
[392] *The Indianapolis News* – November 29, 1898, p.7

Detective Benjamin Thornton

1897-1898 Departmental Photograph

Detectives Jerry Kinney and Ben Thornton received word that Mrs. Daisy Linton, at 444 Agnes Street, had been robbed. They traced the theft to a Barney Stevenson. Following his trail, they found him just before he boarded a train bound for Louisville, Kentucky at Union Station. It was ready to pull out when the detectives arrived. When Stevenson saw Kinney, he started to run, but was caught by Thornton as he ran down the tracks.[393]

Violent Domestic Assault

Miss Katie Johnson, a young woman employed at the Indiana Bicycle Company, found herself being pursued romantically by a fireman with the Big Four railroad named Charles F. Shortridge. He was very persistent but Miss Johnson rejected him several times. He threatened her life if she didn't consent to marriage, one time at the point of a revolver.

On March 4, 1899, Shortridge visited Katie Johnson in her room, at the boarding house at 408 East Ohio Street. He had been banned from visiting the boarding house but managed to slip past the landlady, Mrs. Mary Crow. He tried to kiss Miss Johnson, she objected. Shortridge threw his arms around her.

In one hand was a razor, which he used to slash the left side of her neck, narrowly missing the major arteries. He coolly left the

---

[393] *The Indianapolis News* – December 7, 1898, p.8

rooming house. She was taken to City Hospital in an ambulance. Detectives Kinney, Thornton and John Weible found him on East Washington Street the afternoon of March 5th. Charles F. Shortridge was a police officer for two years some years back.[394]

Charles F. Shortridge appeared in Criminal Court March 23, 1899 on the charge of assault and battery with intent to kill. He pleaded guilty to assault and battery, fined $700 and sentenced to six months in the work house. The punishment was considered light at the time.[395]

Early on the morning of April 24, 1899, Mrs. Daniel Fisher of 117 West Michigan Street, awoke to find a man, who she recognized as John Conn, sitting in a chair at the foot of her bed, going through the pockets of her clothing.

After watching him for two minutes, she screamed for her husband. The man ran out of the room, jumping out one of her

---

394 *The Indianapolis News* – March 6, 1899, p.8

395 *The Indianapolis News* – March 23, 1899, p.6

windows. Conn operated a little shop behind her house. Detective Thornton found him asleep in bed and arrested him. He denied being in her home.[396] John Conn was found guilty of petit larceny.[397]

[396] *The Indianapolis News* – April 24, 1899, p.9
[397] *The Indianapolis News* – May 16, 1899, p.2

CHAPTER 12:
"ALL I ASK IS AN EVEN BREAK"

On the occasion of marking 23 years with the Indianapolis Police Department, Benjamin Thornton wrote a letter to the Editor of *The Indianapolis News*. In part, his remarks were:

"I would like to speak through your paper of the length of service of some of the colored people who are now holding places under the present city administration. Twenty-three years ago today I was appointed a member of the police force, together with five other colored and eight white men. Today there is but one white man on the force, who has served continuously since that time, namely, David Richards.

Of the six colored men, there are two, Carter Temple and myself. These men were put on the department as a trial test, to see how they would compare with the white men. Whether the experiment was a success or a failure, I will leave to the judgment of the good people of this city.

The parties who have had control of these appointments have been more than liberal in their judgments than some of the business men. When they found one that did not come up to the standard, they would let him go and try another. They did not go on the theory that if one failed or was not what was wanted, all were like him and refuse to try another. I could say a great deal more on this subject but will not say anymore.

All that I ask is an even break and a fair show, and we shall demonstrate that we are worthy of all that we are entrusted with.

When I look back and see the little old station house; the small number of men on the force; no telephones or patrol wagon, and think of what we have today, it makes me feel as though I had lived a long time and had seen a great many things. Benjamin T. Thornton

May 24[398]

The home of H.C. Smith, 2115 North Meridian Street was entered the night of June 9th and 13th, 1899. The thief dropped a

---

398 *The Indianapolis News* – May 25, 1899, p.7

red silk handkerchief the second time, which the family recognized as belonging to Harry Boyd, who used to work for them around the house. Boyd lived at 515 Willard Street.

Ben Thornton located Boyd at his home, along with a diamond ring, a watch and cash, all of which were stolen from the home, in his possession.[399] On June 18, 1899, Harry Boyd was found guilty of burglary and petit larceny. He was sentenced to 2-14 years in the Indiana Reformatory.[400]

A boy named Van Johnson, African-American, who was employed as a bellboy at the Denison Hotel, was put on trial in Criminal Court, July 14, 1899. The charge was assault on a white newsboy. The story told in court was that the newsboy was disturbing the people using the Ohio Street entrance of the hotel and that Van Johnson ordered him to leave. The news boy refused to go, claiming that Johnson struck him several times.

Judge Hay happened to be walking by when this occurred and ordered the boys to

---

399 *The Indianapolis News* – June 14, 1899, p.9

400 *The Indianapolis News* – June 19, 1899, p.2

stop fighting and Johnson made an angry retort. The judge took Johnson into custody and sent for Deputy Prosecutor Smith. Judge Hay fined Johnson in his own office. Detective Ben Thornton then furnished bond for the boy.

In court, July 14th, Ben Thornton appeared on behalf of the boy. Thornton began to question Judge Hay, who refused to answer questions asked of them, claiming that Thornton was not an attorney and had no right to interrogate him. Both men became angry, but the court intervened and continued the case until Johnson could get more witnesses.[401]

During the week of August 19, 1899, Mrs. and Mrs. Thornton and their daughter Adelaide visited Chicago. Ben was a delegate to the Afro-American Council there.[402]

Rebecca Allen, a woman living at 630 Superior Street, left home for a short time on September 11, 1899. When she returned, she found a man had broken into her house and

---

[401] *The Indianapolis Journal* – July 15, 1899

[402] *The Indianapolis Recorder* – August 19, 1899

was ransacking it. She chased him out of the house and down the street. Detectives Kinney and Thornton were in the area and joined in the chase when they saw the thief running.

They fired several shots at the fleeing man and finally cornered him in Beck's Livery stable on St. Clair Street. The man gave his name at police headquarters as Robert Franklin, of Nashville, Tennessee. He was recognized as a man released from the work house September 9th, having served a term for petit larceny.[403] Robert Franklin was actually 16 years of age. He pleaded guilty in Criminal Court, October 12, 1899 and sentenced to the Reform School at Plainfield for 1-3 years.[404]

403 *The Indianapolis News* – September 11, 1899, p.1

404 *The Indianapolis News* – October 12, 1899, p.2

Tomlinson Hall

An altercation occurred during a parade of African-American men, celebrating the victory of Mayor Thomas Taggart, October 14, 1899. Among the people in the march was Arthur D. Baxton, age 16. Henry Whitney, a teen, left his job at the English Hotel along with several friends.

They were standing on the curb on Monument Circle. As he marched by the group, Baxton threw a stone, which struck Henry Whitney on the head. Baxton and another boy then assaulted Whitney, hitting him on the wrist with a club.

Henry Whitney ran to the hotel and after the parade was over, went home to 537 East Court Street, got a revolver and went back to Monument Circle via Market Street. While passing Tomlinson Hall, he saw Baxton and some friends sitting. He pulled his revolver and opened fire. The first shot missed Baxton, but the second one struck him in the head. Baxton fell forward on the sidewalk. Whitney fired again and ran away.

One bullet struck Baxton over the left eye, passed around the skull, coming out behind the ear. The other entered just below the left shoulder and couldn't be found. A short time later, Detectives Jerry Kinney and Ben Thornton found Whitney at the English Hotel, where they placed him under arrest.[405] Baxton survived his wounds. Whitney was found guilty and sentenced to 2-14 years at the Indiana Reformatory, November 24, 1899.[406]

A spree of burglaries, committed by four men, had been committed in recent days, in October 1899. The victims included:

---

[405] *The Indianapolis News* – October 14, 1899, p.3

[406] *The Indianapolis News* – November 25, 1899, p.1

Moses Selig, 905 North Capitol Avenue.

Lynn B. Millikan, 2325 North Meridian Street.

Henry Smith, 816 North Illinois Street.

Ben Thornton had a description of the men who had pawned the stolen items, and on October 30th, while sitting in front of the City Market, he spotted them. He called in the rest of the detective force and they surrounded the men, who had started to run between the buildings. After their capture, they were identified as James Jordan, Henry Smith, Albert Hines and Daniel Coffman.[407]

In the middle of November, 1899, a fight occurred where a James Flemming cut Otis Garrett, laying open his scalp and cutting his side. After the fight, Flemming sent this clothing to St. Louis by express and left Indianapolis on a freight train.

Ben Thornton traced his clothing to St. Louis and waited at the express office there until Flemming called for his clothing. Arresting Flemming, he brought him back to Indianapolis the morning of December 4th, on

---

[407] *The Indianapolis News* – October 30, 1899, p.9

a charge of assault and battery with intent to kill.[408]

Ben Thornton's Birthday

On December 18, 1899, Essie Thornton entertained the "Ugly Men's Club" in honor of her husband's 50th birthday. She decorated the home with Christmas greenery, holly and candles. It was a surprise party for Ben Thornton, who entered the house and found his guests assembled.

Essie Thornton had a reputation as an excellent cook and she prepared a birthday cake as her gift to Ben, which was a piece of art, according to *The Indianapolis Recorder*'s account. In the center was a baby doll, typical of an African Prince, being surrounded by candles, an embossed egg containing 50 silver eggs and the monograph of "B.T.T. – 1849-1899" in bass relief.

The menu she prepared consisted of five courses: first, raw oysters with ice; 2nd, turkey with cranberry sauce, spaghetti with cheese, sweet potatoes cooked in brandy, French peas, little pickles and hot light rolls;

---

[408] *The Indianapolis News* – December 4, 1899, p.9

3rd, chicken salad, Zepherettes, stuffed olives and almonds; 4th, Ice cream and cake, snapping bon bons; 5th, candles and cigars.[409]

Another rash of homes being stripped of their fixtures was going on in the new year of 1900. Following a clue, Detectives Splan and Thornton left for Ingalls, Indiana, where they tracked down Edward Monroe and Grant Watkins, who they said had been responsible for wrecking the interior of vacant homes throughout Indianapolis.[410]

Once back in Indianapolis with the suspects, four more boys in the gang were rounded up: Henry Russell, Wilbur Carter, Julius Moore and George Cowherd. Thornton and Splan rounded them up the morning of January 24th. They were charged with breaking into vacant houses and cutting out the plumbing and gas fixtures.

Detectives Splan and Thornton said that these boys belonged to two separate gangs. Several sacks of stolen goods were

---

[409] *The Indianapolis Recorder* – December 23, 1899

[410] *The Indianapolis News* – January 22, 1900, p.9

brought to the police station from junk shops.[411]

On February 5, 1900, the six boys were found guilty and committed to the Reform School for boys. George Cowherd, had his sentence suspended.[412]

One of Ben Thornton's stranger cases occurred on February 26, 1900 in front of a second hand clothing store at 417 East Washington Street. For a half hour, Thomas Duncan inspected a dummy (mannequin), wearing a $6 coat and vest.

A witness watched long enough while Duncan fumbled with the buttons on the dummy's clothing, to call the police. Ben Thornton and Timothy Splan arrived as Duncan took the clothes off the "dummy" and then disappeared up a stairway. The detectives caught him.[413] He was sentenced to 1-3 years in the Jeffersonville Reformatory.[414]

Ben Thornton gave an address to the Propagandist Club last night on "How to

---

411 *The Indianapolis News* – January 24, 1900, p.9
412 *The Indianapolis News* – February 6, 1900, p.8
413 *The Indianapolis News* – February 27, 1900, p.9
414 *The Indianapolis News* – February 28, 1900, p.8

Succeed." His talk concentrated on honesty and integrity as the means by which success is attained.[415] Ben made a trip to Peoria, Illinois in March, returning March 28th. It was for private business.[416]

Counterfeiting Ring on Indiana Avenue

On the day Ben Thornton returned to Indianapolis, counterfeit silver dollars had started flooding the northwestern part of town. Nearly all of the merchants along Indiana Avenue, as far as Fall Creek, were victims.

Ben and Timothy Splan were placed on the case and got descriptions of the three men who were passing the coins. They followed a number of clues, until March 29th, when the suspects were spotted.

The suspects moved their operations from the northwest side to West Indianapolis, where merchants began receiving counterfeits. Merchants on West Washington Street began receiving them, so the detectives split up, to cover a wider territory.

---

[415] *The Indianapolis News* – March 23, 1900, p.1

[416] *The Indianapolis News* – March 29, 1900, p.1

At 10:30 p.m. on March 29, 1900, Detective Splan saw three men at South West Street who answered the description of the suspects. He shadowed them for some time. They went near Holmes' Saloon, at West and Chesapeake Streets, where one went inside. When he came out, Splan entered the saloon and told the bartender to put aside the dollar he had accepted, to be used as evidence.

The men split up at Washington Street. Splan caught two of them and put them in the custody of the firemen at No. 6 engine house. He found the third man not far away. They were named George Ellis of St. Louis, Ed Kelly of Louisville and Harry Young, of Iowa. They were turned over to the Federal authorities.[417]

In the spring of 1900, Ben Thornton planted a bed of violets in in the yard of his home.[418]

In April of 1900, Ben Thornton and Archie Greathouse, saloon keeper, began

---

417 *The Indianapolis News* – March 30, 1900, p.4

418 *The Indianapolis News* – November 17, 1900, p.9

erecting a flat at the corner of Bright and Walnut Streets.[419]

Indianapolis Police received a message that Noel Winston, who burglarized several tailor shops in Indianapolis several months previous, had been arrested in Springfield, Ohio. Ben Thornton left for Ohio on the afternoon of May 2, 1900, to retrieve him.[420]

As the 24th anniversary of Benjamin Thornton's employment with the Indianapolis Police Department arrived on May 24, 1900, *The Indianapolis News* said that in point of service, he was probably the oldest (longest serving) "colored" policeman in the world. It went on to say that Carter Temple, who retired one month earlier, joined the force with Thornton.[421]

Stolen Bicycle Investigation

Detectives Timothy Splan and Ben Thornton arrested a man named Bert Whitsell on May 28, 1900 for stealing 14 bicycles, three sets of harness and some pigs, which they recovered at the house of Samuel

---

419 *The Indianapolis News* – April 20, 1900, p.11
420 *The Indianapolis News* – May 2, 1900, p.3
421 *The Indianapolis News* – May 24, 1900, p.3

Reckard, in the Wolf Pike.[422] Samuel Reckard gave information on who had been selling him the stolen bicycles.

At 3 a.m., May 29th, Captain Jerry Kinney and Detectives Thornton, Timothy Splan, Thomas F. Dugan and David R. Lancaster drove to the farm of Harry Bratton Hall, 15 miles northeast of Indianapolis and arrested him. The son of a prominent farmer, young Hall was found with a stolen bicycle in his possession.

The detectives next visited the farm of Claude Dawson, near the Hamilton County line and recovered a stolen bicycle from him. He was also arrested. This investigation was done under poor weather conditions, and Ben contracted a bad cold.[423] [424]

Samuel Reckard, Bert Whitsell, Harry Hall and Claud Dawson were tried by Judge Alford on charges of bicycle stealing. Whitesell, Hall and Dawson stole the bicycles and sold them to Reckard. Reckard and Hall were sentenced to six months in the work

---

422 *The Indianapolis News* – May 28, 1900, p.3

423 *The Indianapolis News* – May 29, 1900, p.1

424 *The Indianapolis News* – June 19, 1900, p.5

house, while Dawson and Whitesell, both under age, received 30 days, suspended.[425]

The third Annual Session of the National Afro American Council was scheduled to be held in Indianapolis, during August of 1900. Benjamin Thornton was assigned to the General Committee for this council, as of June 16, 1900.[426] This would be his third time to attend this session.

425 *The Indianapolis News* – June 26, 1900, p.8

426 The Colored American – June 16, 1900, p.4

CHAPTER 13:
BEN THORNTON'S LAST CASE

The last criminal case that Benjamin T. Thornton was assigned began in Cleveland, Ohio on May 6, 1900. At 8:30 p.m., Patrolman John Shipp of the Cleveland Police Department and his partner Charles Dangler, were sent to 23 Charles Street for a burglary in progress.

As Patrolman Shipp went under a pantry window, a burglar leaned out and shot him three times. Shipp was hit in the jugular vein, the right side of his back below his ribs and in the left leg, above the knee. Mortally wounded, he staggered to his partner and said, "I'm shot, Charley."

The burglar climbed out a front window of the house and fled, shooting at bystanders as he left the scene. He dropped his .32 revolver as he did so.[427] It was later determined that the man who murdered Patrolman Shipp was Edward Ruthven. He had been arrested in Bucyrus, Ohio in April 1900 and escaped two weeks later.

---

[427] Ibid.

On May 7th, Cleveland police had traced the suspect to a home at Central Avenue and Greenwood Street and after calling for him to surrender; he opened up an upstairs window and began firing at police with two revolvers. Police returned fire. He jumped from a second story window and ran down an alley, turning to fire frequently as he did. Over 50 shots were exchanged.[428] It was believed Ruthven was wounded several times in this gun battle.

A reward of $1,000 was offered for the capture of Edward Ruthven. A citizen of Indianapolis named Cornelius Jackson, informed Benjamin Thornton that he was in Indianapolis and holed up at 1118 Lafayette Street, on the near northwest part of town. Ben was assigned to the case. For a number of nights, he staked out the 1118 Lafayette Street address, where Ruthven was said to occasionally stop.

The weather was bad and while out in the rain these evenings, the cold he already had contracted grew worse. Since the middle of May, a 20-year long asthmatic condition returned. It was a severe attack. Ben went

[428] The Allentown Leader – May 8, 1900, p.5

home, sick. His doctor was able to get him some relief.

For years, Dr. Blanchard Pettijohn had treated him for his asthma and Ben had consulted noted physicians around the United States about the condition. For several days he didn't appear at headquarters.

Ben went back out and watched the Lafayette Street address the nights of May 31st and June 1st. The rain came down in "torrents", according to *The Indianapolis News*.[429] He stuck to his post, becoming so ill he was ordered home. He left to go home on the 2nd. On that day, June 2, 1900, Cornelius Jackson advised the detective office that Edward Ruthven had returned to 1118 Lafayette Street.

Captain Kinney called a number of his men together and started for the house in a patrol wagon. On the way they met Ben Thornton, who was on his way home and insisted on going along with them. Captain Kinney, knowing how sick Ben Thornton

[429] *The Indianapolis News* – June 20, 1900, p.7

was, would not allow him to do so. He told him to go home.[430] [431]

COTTAGE IN WHICH "BAD ED" RUTHVEN MADE HIS LAST FIGHT

1118 Lafayette Street, Indianapolis, [432]

The detectives surrounded the house and went in through the front and back at the same time. Ruthven came out the front door, coming face to face with Captain Kinney and several of his men, with their

---

430 *The Indianapolis Journal* – November 25, 1900

431 *The Indianapolis Journal* – June 19, 1900.

432 *The Indianapolis News* – April 30, 1910, p.15

revolvers drawn. The police forced their way inside the house.

Ruthven pulled the trigger of his own revolver, but Kinney managed to get his finger stuck in the trigger guard, preventing it from being fired. Detective Samuel Gerber saw this and fearing for Captain Kinney's life, shot Ruthven once. He was taken to City Hospital, two men guarding him 24 hours a day for a long while.[433]

Ben protested about not being able to participate in the capture of Edward Ruthven. Ben Thornton's health had begun to fail at last. His asthmatic condition developed about June 9th into a case of acute pneumonia of his left lung. The reports that were sent back to IPD headquarters indicated his illness was not a serious one however.

On June 18, 1900, Ben Thornton died at 11:30 p.m. at his home, 525 Bright Street of pneumonia. It was agreed by all news accounts that his death was caused by being exposed to the elements for long hours during his wait for Edward Ruthven to

---

433 *The Indianapolis News* – June 28, 1901

appear.[434] *The Indianapolis-Recorder* wrote "The illness that preceded his death was in a great measure due to the zealous performance of his duties."[435]

The death of Ben Thornton was unexpected and met with widespread grief and shock by his co-workers and the citizens of Indianapolis – with the exception certainly of the criminal elements of the town.

A memorial service in his honor was called for Thursday, June 21st at 2 p.m. at Bethel A.M.E. Church. His body lay in state at his home, from 5 p.m. Wednesday to 12:30 a.m. Thursday. It was viewed by thousands of people.

Numerous floral offerings were presented, one of the most prominent having a design in the shape of a policeman's star shaped badge, four feet high and 34" wide, which the Indianapolis Police Department

---

[435] *The Indianapolis News* – June 19, 1900

sent. Ben always liked the star and crescent design and owned a jewel in this shape set with diamonds. This was the design IPD by the detective force.

Other tributes came from the Ugly Men's club, the Lincoln Union lodge and the Patriarche, the Household of Ruth, the Pride of the West Lodge of the Knights of Pythias and Mr. Archie Greathouse, who was a friend of Ben.

The pall bearers for Ben Thornton were Captain Jeremiah Kinney and Detective Timothy Splan of the detective force, Patrolmen Edward Harris and David Richards, Dr. B.J. Morgan of the Ugly Men's Club, N.Hill and C.A. Webb of the Lincoln Union lodge and Benjamin Wade and Edmund White of the Patriarchie.

IPD Pall bearers for Benjamin Thornton

Clockwise, from top left: **Timothy Splan, Jerry Kinney, David Richards, Edward Harris**

His funeral procession left Odd Fellow's Hall on Indiana Avenue at 1:20 p.m. It was headed by a detail of 24 patrolmen, under the command of Captain Christian Kruger. They were followed by the Indianapolis Military band, the Uniformed Patriarche, then the lodges and the Household of Ruth. It was described as one of the largest funeral processions seen in Indianapolis in many years.

The services at Bethel A.M.E. Church were conducted by the Reverend C.W. Newton, assisted by visiting ministers. The burial was at Crown Hill Cemetery.[436]

The tombstone of Benjamin and Essie Thornton, is located in Crown Hill Cemetery, Indianapolis, Indiana. The location is in section 38, lot 241.

The Indianapolis News gave an analysis of Benjamin Thornton's characteristics as a detective. He made the acquaintance of all classes of people to further his investigations and he learned the method of operation, known to police now as the criminal's "M.O." to such an extent, that

[436] *The Indianapolis Recorder* – June 23, 1900

he was "seldom baffled". He had records of well-known thieves and criminals on the tip of his tongue and knew them on sight.[437]

As stated by *The Indianapolis News*, "Thornton was possessed of a remarkable courage. Many a time he walked into places where it seemed that he would meet death, but with the exception of being wounded a few times, he escaped serious injury. He had many narrow escapes from death, but he took all of them as a matter of little consequence. Thornton was known as a fighter who never considered the odds against him, and the bullies and toughs about the city who were looking for trouble always gave him a wide berth. He successfully solved several mysterious murder cases during his experience as a detective, and recovered thousands of dollars, worth of stolen property." [438]

At his death, Ben Thornton was a charter member of the Lincoln Union Lodge of "colored" Odd Fellows, having served for several years as their secretary. When he died, he was the grand director of the

---

[437] *The Indianapolis News* – June 20, 1900, p.7

[438] Ibid.

biennial movable committee, having been elected at St. Louis in 1898 to serve a second term. He was also a member of the Pride of the West Lodge, Knights of Pythias.

George W. Powell, former superintendent of police remarked, "While I was connected with the police department I considered Detective Thornton one of the best, if not the most efficient officer on the force. He was a man of the utmost integrity, and with one exception was the best educated man on the force. His reports to me were models of grammatical construction. I have found his fame has spread all over the country, thereby lifting the standard of our whole police force. In my opinion his place should be filled by an intelligent colored man, for there is work in the police department that none but a colored man can do."[439]

The informant, Cornelius Jackson, age 35, was informed by IPD that he had $500 of the $1000 reward money coming to him. On June 18th, Captain Kinney handed him $500 and Johnson returned $250 back, asking that

---

[439] Ibid.

it be divided between the detectives who assisted in the capture of Ruthven.

Estimates vary, but on that same day, either 5 minutes, 30 minutes or several hours later, Jackson died in the basement of Huder's drug store, on East Washington Street.[440] On his person was found $25.96 at the morgue. He lived with his family at 1134 Lafayette Street.[441]

Edward Ruthven reportedly enjoyed hearing about the deaths of informant Cornelius Jackson and Benjamin Thornton. He himself was convicted of the murder of Patrolman John Shipp. Ruthven was electrocuted in the Ohio State penitentiary, June 21, 1901.[442]

---

[440] *The Indianapolis News* – November 26, 1900, p.1

[441] *The Indianapolis News* – June 20, 1900, p.7

Edward Ruthven [443]

443 http://www.drc.ohio.gov/web/executed/large/executed10.jpg

A Bed of Violets

In November of 1900, the bed of violets that Ben Thornton had planted in his yard the previous spring was in full bloom for the second time. On the morning of November 17th, Essie Thornton gathered a bunch of the violets and decorated a photograph of her late husband.[444]

After the death of Benjamin T. Thornton, who was generally recognized in Indianapolis, as well as many areas in the United States as an excellent detective, white or African-American, it was discussed within the Indianapolis Police Department about finding a suitable replacement of the same race.

In December of 1903, Patrolman Benjamin W. Lee, an African-American, was discussed in *The Indianapolis News* as having detective ability. He had benefited the detective department numerous times for the past month, passing on tips on criminals in the African-American community that had led to successful prosecutions.

---

[444] *The Indianapolis News* – November 17, 1900, p.9

A member of the department for four years at that point, Lee's ambition was to fill the shoes of Ben Thornton.[445] In February of 1906 however, the Chief of Police Metzger leveled charges of unbecoming without specifics, against Patrolman Lee, who left the force.

On October 18, 1906, a letter to the Editor of *The Indianapolis News* was printed, which succinctly stated the problem with not having an African-American on the detective squad. This same analysis would be given by superiors within IPD for many years to come.[446]

---

[445] *The Indianapolis News* – December 12, 1903, p.19

[446] *The Indianapolis News* – October 18, 1906, p.8

COLORED DETECTIVE WANTED.

To The Indianapolis Star:

The death of no officer, however proficient and highly honored he may have been, destroys the need of that particular officer, and no man ever filled an office that another man of his own class could not fill if necessary. It has often occurred to me that a grave mistake was made in not filling the position of a colored detective made vacant by the death of our most faithful and successful Benjamin Thornton, most especially so since the escape of Coe.

I notice in your comment on the successful work of Jacob Kurtz among the criminal element of our race you attribute his success to the fact that he has associated so long and familiarly with colored people that he really knows us and can sympathize and gain the confidence of the bad ones. Now, does it not stand to reason that a colored man, who naturally had sympathy for and knowledge of his race, could fill the place more ably? The fact that Benjamin Thornton was made a detective and retained that office so long proves that there was need of a colored detective, and, properly trained, he could beat every one else catching the lawbreakers of our race.

The argument may be advanced that Benjamin Thornton's successor has not been found, and it is highly probable he has not been thoroughly searched for. He is somewhere in the race in Indianapolis, and he is needed, and should be found.

MARY B. HITCHENS.

Indianapolis, Oct. 16.

Indianapolis would not see another African-American detective until May of 1918, when George Sneed, newly appointed to IPD, was promoted to Detective Sergeant. He was a good choice and made a reputation nearly equal to Benjamin Thornton for his detective skills. He was also the first Black to be promoted to the rank of Sergeant and Lieutenant (1926). He remained a detective until 1947 when he moved over to the Vice Squad.

Essie (Moore) Thornton

Mrs. Essie M. Thornton lived as a widow in her double at 533-535 Bright Street, with her daughter Addie. This home is now the site of a part of the IUPUI campus. She was a member of the Daughters of Charity, which she helped found in 1895 and a devoted member of the Bethel A.M.E. Church. She operated her catering business through 1904.

What little of her family that is known is that she attended the funeral services of unnamed sisters in Kansas City and Butte, Montana in the month of May, 1902. She had a niece named Mrs. Essie M. Hill (1884-1970) who was born in Denver, Colorado and died in Los Angeles, California, wife of John Hill and later, Percy Armstead (1892-1974). Essie M. Thornton had a first cousin named Will Wright who lived in Chicago, 1912.

She suffered a stroke in 1911 and was confined to her home for the last year of her life. Essie died at home, September 26, 1912 and was buried by Benjamin's side.[447]

---

[447] The Freeman – October 5, 1912, p.8

1907 High School Graduation Photograph

Adelaide D. (Thornton) Riley

Adelaide D. Thornton was born Esther Mosby, May 20, 1888 and adopted in 1891 by Benjamin and Essie (Moore) Thornton. She figured prominently in a mandamus suit which was covered by many newspapers across the United States, in 1894-1895. She was given musical instruction at an early age and gave her first known public performance February 24, 1900 at a surprise birthday party for former Representative John A. Puryear.

She was very involved in the affairs of the Bethel A.M.E. Church, serving as recording secretary for its Junior Christian Endeavor Society in March 1903. On August 12, 1905 she was elected Vice-President of this organization. In 1907, she graduated from Shortridge High School.

She was elected to the Music Committee of the Treble Cleff Club, September 6, 1909 and as a recent graduate of the Leckner Music School, obtained a position as a pianist for the Robert Gould Shaw School, September 25, 1909.

The Indianapolis Recorder described Adelaide on April 22, 1911 as "the city's finest pianist." In July of 1914, Adelaide

Thornton was attending the Conservatory of Music in Chicago.[448]

In 1919, Ellen Thomas Meriwether and Adelaide Thornton Riley founded the Indianapolis Music Promoters (IMP), as a branch of the National Association of Negro Musicians (NANM). This was established after they attended an organizational meeting of the national association in Washington, D.C. The stated purpose of the club was to encourage its members to study music and to encourage musical talent among the youth.[449] They are still an active organization.

Adelaide, now the music supervisor in what was called "the Colored Schools of Indianapolis Public schools", attended the National Association of Music supervisors that convened at the Stevens hotel in Chicago, in March 1930.[450] Adelaide wrote a thesis in 1940, titled "The Junior High

---

[448] *The Indianapolis Recorder* – July 18, 1914.

[449] http://www.indianahistory.org/our-collections/collection-guides/indianapolis-music-promoters-collection-1903-1977.pdf

[450] *The Indianapolis Recorder* – April 4, 1930.

School Music Teachers and Some Problems They May Encounter."[451]

Adelaide continued her education, graduating from Butler University in June of 1931. In 1941, she received her Master's Degree in Music Education at the Arthur Jordan Conservatory of Music. She married, Hurlburt Therkield Riley, an educator as well. Adelaide taught school at School No. 36, 2801 North Capitol Avenue and School No. 37, 2425 East 25th Street.

They lived at 2712 North Capitol Avenue in a house built about 1929. She became seriously ill in 1947. She retired in 1953 and passed away October 21, 1954 at home. She was buried in Crown Hill Cemetery, section 38, lot 241.

---

[451] Worldcat

Hurlburt T. Riley - 1915

[452] Adelaide in 1924

[452] Activities of the Indianapolis Chamber of Commerce, March 1924, Vol. 38, No. 3 p.15

www.ingramcontent.com/pod-product-compliance
Lightning Source LLC
LaVergne TN
LVHW051447080426
835509LV00017B/1691
9780692072400